Successful group work

The Transferable and Learning Skills Series

Series editors:

Anne Hilton, Manager, Student Learning Development Centre, Library, De Montfort University
Sue Robinson, Editor, Student Learning Development Centre, Library, De Montfort University

Job hunting after university or college, Jan Perrett
Research skills, Brian Allison, Tim O'Sullivan, Alun Owen, Arthur Rothwell, Jenny Rice, Carol Saunders
Successful group work, Simon Rogerson, Tim O'Sullivan, Jenny Rice, Carol Saunders

THE TRANSFERABLE AND LEARNING SKILLS SERIES

Successful group work

Time management **Simon Rogerson**
Managing your learning
Working in groups
Managing your group project
Jenny Rice
Carol Saunders
Tim O'Sullivan

**KOGAN
PAGE**

First published in 1996

Kogan Page Limited
120 Pentonville Road
London N1 9JN

© De Montfort University, 1996

British Library Cataloguing in Publication Data
A CIP record for this book is available from the British Library
ISBN 0 7494 1867 2

Design and typesetting by Paul Linnell, De Montfort University
Printed and bound in Great Britain by Biddles Ltd, Guildford and King's Lynn

Contents

Part C: Working in groups 54

Part D: Managing your group project 82

Part A: Time management

Introduction

This first part of the book aims to make you aware of how to use your time more effectively through proper analysis and planning. We can all be more effective in using our time. A little forethought and planning can dramatically increase the time you have available to do the things that are important to you. You are likely to discover there are many ways to be more effective, but changing your habits can be difficult, so do not be overambitious in expecting to double your effectiveness overnight. It might be better to try to modify one habit at a time rather than trying to adopt a completely new way of working in one go. Evolution will be more acceptable and sustainable than an apocalyptic approach.

Objectives

At the end of the exercises in this part you should be able to:
- undertake a self-examination of your work and leisure time;
- establish a set of long-term personal goals;
- analyse the allocation of your time;
- identify and implement a suitable time management strategy.

This part has been designed so that you can work at your own pace. You will need time to reflect and collect data. This reflection time will be identified. You will be presented with ideas about time management and invited to consider questions and scenarios in order to consolidate your knowledge and ensure you really understand the underpinning concepts.

1 Introduction to time management

In this chapter you will consider what time means to you and identify some ways in which you might manage it more effectively. If you are to become an effective manager of your time you must first understand the nature of what you are attempting to manage.

 Activity 1.1

Time can be defined as a finite duration as distinct from eternity, but is this useful in the context of your studies and leisure?

Spend about ten minutes writing down some ideas of what time means to you. The following words and phrases may help you to focus your thoughts:
- at the same time
- on time
- at times
- time off
- from time to time
- timeless
- in no time
- timely
- in time

Note: The clearer your understanding of what you mean by time, the more effective you will be at organising yourself.

Have you now got a clearer idea of time? This can be quite difficult to achieve because time is an intangible concept. Time is a paradox; you never have enough time but you have all the time that is available. Time is a resource, but if you do not use it, it will disappear. You cannot increase the quantity of time you receive but you can ensure that you use it on the things that are important to you.

Activity 1.2

In the scenario below, Peter appears to have difficulty in achieving his goals. Identify what the problems are and suggest ways in which he might overcome them.

Scenario

Peter always started the day with coffee from the machine on the sixth floor. It was a chance to catch up with the gossip. Today was no exception, but, 'Where is everyone?' he thought, 'It's only 9.20.' Just then Iram arrived. He remembered the chat they had had last week. 'Wonder if she got that job?' he thought.

One hour later, Peter left for the library. He now knew that Iram had not got the job and she felt very upset by the situation, believing that she had been used by the company.

His major assignment was still only half written. It was now nearly 11.00 and he had a tutorial at 12.00. 'Maybe I'd better do that reading from yesterday's lecture and tackle the assignment straight after lunch,' he thought.

Peter's tutorial with Dr Underwood finished just before lunch. Lunch was fun, it always was on a Wednesday when Mary, Paul and himself met up. Feeling somewhat light headed, he returned to the library, thinking 'Why do we have to do that assignment anyway? It's not very relevant.' Looking over the briefing for completing the assignment made him more convinced of the futility of the exercise.

He was close to getting something written, when Ravinder appeared. 'Hello Peter,' Ravinder began, 'how did the tutorial go this morning? Was Underwood in a mood as usual?'

'You can say that again!' Peter retorted. And so the discussion started. Ravinder sat down and exchanged a few words with his friend. By the time Ravinder left it was 3.15 and Peter had decided to sort out a few small items and get on with that important assignment the next morning. 'After all,' he told himself, 'tomorrow is another day.'

Did you manage to identify what Peter was doing wrong in the scenario? There are several issues to consider. Here are some of the more significant ones:

Issue	How to be more effective
Peter starts work late	Get off to a flying start each day and allocate some quiet time each day
He puts off jobs he does not like	Determine to do the most difficult or least exciting jobs sooner rather than later
Peter allows himself to be interrupted by himself and others	Develop stronger will-power and stick to a schedule
All activities seem to have equal priority	Identify the important activities and focus on these
Little has been achieved in the day	Aim to achieve one major task each day

Managing time

As you have now discovered, time is a *personal concept* which means there is no right or wrong perception of time. Learning to manage time requires commitment which, in the scenario, Peter found hard to give. The difficulty is how you approach various activities. Your approach will be influenced by the assumptions you make about the nature of your work and the environment in which you live and work. Some assumptions will generally be more useful than others for managing your time effectively.

Time management is simply a way of using time effectively. Working faster or working longer are poor strategies for managing time. It is more sensible to identify your priority activities and concentrate on those. These activities will depend on your changing values and perceptions. Managing time is about managing yourself. It is about adapting to a given situation so that you can get the most out of your time. For you to do this, you must accept that you can influence and ultimately control the environment in which you live and work. You must learn to spend your time wisely.

 Activity 1.3

Do you think the following statements are true or false?

a Most students are overworked because of the nature of their studies.
b Your work is unique and not subject to repetitive patterns.
c No one ever has enough time.
d Most people can find ways of saving time.
e Managing time is simply a case of reducing time on certain activities.

f   Scheduling 'quiet time' is impossible.
g   You can solve most time problems by working harder.
h   People who concentrate on working efficiently are the most effective.
i   Most of the ordinary day-to-day activities do not need to be planned.
j   It is not always possible to work on the basis of priorities.
k   Identifying a problem is easy, it is deciding upon a solution which is hard.
l   You know how you spend your time and can easily identify your biggest time wasters.
m   Controlling your time means that you miss unexpected opportunities.
n   Time management denies spontaneity.
o   It is not necessary to write down your objectives.

 Activity 1.3 – solution

a   False. It is the nature of the person and not the nature of the studies. Overwork is often caused by failing to establish priorities, spending too much time on unnecessary detail and having a poor work ethic.
b   False. All work has patterns. The problem is identifying the form of the pattern. Once identified you can schedule your time more effectively.
c   False. You have all the time there is. There is always enough time to do what is really important. The problem is deciding what is important.
d   False. There is no way to save time. All you can do is spend it. The concept of saving time really means reducing time on one activity so you can use it on another.
e   False. Managing time is about spending an appropriate amount of time on each activity.
f   False. You can always find a quiet period to concentrate on the very important activities. The problem is removing the likelihood of distractions and interruptions.
g   False. Working harder does not always mean working more effectively. Stress, tension and fatigue will take their toll.
h   False. Efficiency is about doing things right but effectiveness is about doing the right things.
i   False. The ordinary day-to-day activities need to be planned very carefully as it is these which can use up most of your time and if unplanned cause each day to become very hectic.
j   False. Not only is it possible to do this but it is essential if you are going to be an effective time manager.
k   False. Identifying the problem is probably the greatest obstacle of all in effective time management.
l   False. Few people know how they spend their time. Your working

5

pattern tends to be habitual and if not periodically reviewed can continue to include habits which waste much time.

m False. If you manage your time well you will have time to follow up the unexpected.

n False. Managing your time will leave you with unscheduled periods which can be held in reserve to compensate for the spontaneous activities which you get involved in.

o False. The action of writing down your objectives clarifies them, makes them visible and increases your commitment to them.

Assess yourself as follows:

- **14–15 correct answers**
  Excellent, you are making good use of your time.
- **12–13 correct answers**
  Good, you are becoming an effective manager of time.
- **10–11 correct answers**
  Fair, but you had better review your working methods soon.
- **Fewer than 10 correct**
  Unsatisfactory, your ideas of time management appear ineffective.

How did you score? Did you disagree with some of the general conclusions? If not then you should be able to become an effective time manager. If you did then you should carefully consider your attitude and why you are taking a particular stance. Are your assumptions realistic for the environment in which you live and work?

 Activity 1.4

Copy out the headings and boxes from page 23 and draw an additional eight boxes. In your table, write down ten steps which you believe are essential if you are to manage your time effectively. As you work through this programme of self-study you will be asked to review these steps, modifying them and adding additional ones to reflect your growing awareness of time management.

Note: Some general pointers will be provided later.

Remember: Time is a uniquely personal concept and learning to manage time requires personal commitment.

It is worth taking a break now before you start Chapter 2. **Do not look at page 12.**

2   Self-examination of work and leisure time

Now you have some idea of what time means to you, you are going to review your work and leisure activities. This will provide you with some short-term time management pointers and lay the foundation for a long-term strategy. If you are going to succeed in your studies and enjoy your leisure, you must know what things you *have* to do and *want* to do, and how long they are likely to take. You must be aware of the obstacles that are likely to hinder you in achieving your pre-defined objectives.

Things to be done

Most people have things waiting to be done when there is time and you will be no exception. However, do you have a clear picture of what these things are? The things you need to do when you have time are not all equally important. Some will have higher priority than others. You need to be aware of this if you are to become an effective time manager.

 Activity 2.1

Use the sample form on page 23 to list all your outstanding activities to which you should devote more time, as they will have a positive effect on your work and leisure once instigated. Write them down in the order you think of them. They can be large or small and almost anything. Now rank these activities into an order of priority using the column marked 'Priority'.

Now make a list of your five most important activities, following the style of the form on page 23. Give brief reasons why you have allocated each activity its high priority.

Decide how much time you need to complete each activity. Where it is a one-off activity, estimate the total time required. Where it is a continuous activity, estimate the time you need each week. Record these estimates in the 'Time' column. Set yourself a target when each activity should be finished and record this in the 'Date' column.

Obstacles

You probably have some idea of what prevents you from doing the things that you believe are important. Have you got these reasons for non-achievement well documented and are they valid reasons? If you are going to make effective use of your time you need to know precisely what distracts you from achieving some predefined objective.

Activity 2.2

You have defined the five most important activities which are outstanding. Carefully analyse each activity in turn and try to identify all the reasons why you have yet to start, let alone finish, these activities which are so important to you. Turn to page 23 and copy out the form, giving yourself five 'Obstacle' boxes. As each reason is identified, write it down.

Now write down a reason why each of the obstacles you have listed exists. Rank all the obstacles in order of importance, recording your order in the column 'Priority'.

Draw a new form, similar to that on page 24, and transfer the five most significant obstacles to this form. Consider how you might overcome them. Record your ideas in the space provided. You will consider obstacles in more detail in Chapter 5, pages 16–17.

You now have quite a detailed picture of what you should concentrate your efforts on and how your efforts are likely to be thwarted. Such knowledge is the foundation of good time management.

Estimating

Do you know how long it takes you to do things? How accurate are you at estimating activity durations? You probably have a rough idea, but what is it based upon? How feasible do you think the durations and targets are that you set in Activity 2.1?

You must try to be realistic when estimating. It is very common to underestimate rather than overestimate and, if you miss deadlines because of this, you will become disheartened. Consider similar activities you have done before and try to remember how long they took. Set yourself realistic target dates. Take account of the obstacles you are likely to encounter when trying to achieve targets.

You will be more accurate if you break an activity into its constituent parts. For example, to produce a 3,000-word essay for a coursework assignment is likely to involve you in: planning, research and data collection, analysis and idea consolidation, writing the first draft and subsequent modifications and, finally, preparation and presentation of the finished essay. By considering each sub-activity in turn you are more likely to understand the nature of the work to be undertaken and how long it is going to take you.

A working system

Completing the simple exercises in Activity 2.1 and Activity 2.2 has enabled you to compile some key information about activities and obstacles.

- which activities are waiting to be done;
- which activities are most important;
- the reasons why activities have not been completed;
- how obstacles might be overcome;
- how much time is needed to complete activities;
- when activities will be completed.

So, you now have a simple system that can reveal why you have not achieved what you wanted to do.

Remember:
- it is possible to use your time better;
- you can improve your performance using a simple system to identify priorities and obstacles;
- such a system does not take much time itself;
- time management is about thinking beforehand to ensure you are always *doing the right thing*.

Take a break and reflect on what you have learnt in this chapter. In the Chapter 3 you are going to consider how your personality influences how and when you undertake the activities you have just listed. In Chapter 4 you will learn how to provide a focus for your activities by defining personal goals.

3 Self-analysis

The better you know yourself the easier it is to set personal goals. If you spend some time on self-analysis you will become more aware of what you like and what you do not like, what is important to you and what is not. You will then be in a position to identify where to direct your efforts, which is itself the foundation of a long-term personal plan.

Working

You are likely to have an opinion of how well you work, but have you ever considered this in detail? Such critical self-analysis can prove very beneficial.

 Activity 3.1

Carefully consider each question and answer either 'seldom', 'sometimes' or 'often' for each. Answer as honestly as possible.

a   Do you spend six to eight hours working?
b   Do you spend time on the important tasks?
c   Do you often waste time chatting?
d   Do you use your initiative or wait to be directed?
e   Do you keep to what you have promised?
f   Can you work effectively for long periods?
g   Do you work well in the morning?
h   Do you work well in the evening?
i   Do you work well under pressure?
j   Do you adapt to the needs of others when working in teams?
k   Do you persevere with difficult tasks?
l   Do you enjoy your studies?

Look at this profile. Are there any areas of concern? *Do you think that you work in a way which suits you?*

Influences

Throughout your life, at home, at work and at leisure, you will have been subjected to many influences. Such influences impact on the way you think and behave today and on what you consider to be important. Being aware of this background will help you to plan for the future and help you make most effective use of your time.

Activity 3.2

Consider what has influenced the way you behave in leisure and in your studies. In each broad area note down whether the influence has been negative, neutral or positive and then add any major items which have caused this influence.

    a Inherited characteristics
    b Environment
    c Education
    d Work experience
    e Attitude of self and others
    f Motivation
    g Successes and failures
    h Self-development

The information you have collected in Activity 3.1 and Activity 3.2 is valuable to you. It should enable you to focus on the issues that you have to address if you are going to be more effective in the way you operate. For example, in Activity 3.2 a negative influence in your environment might have been your overreliance on a parent to get you up and off to school in the morning when you were a young teenager. You might have stated in Activity 3.1 that you do not work well in the morning, rarely attending that 9.00 am lecture on the topic you least like. Your response in Activity 3.1 may be partly due to the influence stated in Activity 3.2. Having highlighted the problem, you can now consider how to overcome this other than by installing a telephone for a parental early morning call service!

Self-awareness

You have now spent some time considering how you work and the underlying reasons for this behaviour. There will be strong points on which to build and weaker points which require some attention. Such knowledge will enable you to be more effective in managing your time.

 ## *Activity 3.3*

Now review and, if appropriate, modify your response to Activity 1.4.

Caught in the act!

If you are reading this having just finished Chapter 1, you were told not to.

Interrupting yourself is a classic problem associated with effective time management.

4 Long-term personal goals

It is not easy to define your personal goals. A goal should motivate you to take action and provide some focus for your efforts. The following points should help you define meaningful goals.

- Goals should be your own, conceived and achieved by you.
- Goals should be written down.
- Goals should be realistic and achievable.
- Goals should be precise and measurable.
- Goals should have a time frame.
- Goals should be compatible with one another.

The goals you define should encompass both work and leisure. It is only when you have an idea of what you want to do with your life that you can decide what you have to spend your time on.

 Activity 4.1

In your notebook, define your five most important personal goals. Use the guidelines above to check that each one is meaningful.

Key areas

Having established your goals, you need to identify the main areas within which you need to use your time and concentrate your efforts. These will be your key areas. You should restrict the number of key areas to a maximum of nine, otherwise the span will become too large for you to keep all areas in focus. Typically, your key areas might subdivide into intellectual activity, work activity, family and leisure. Some generalised examples of key areas are as follows:

Intellectual activity:
- course modules
- evening classes
- course project
- reading.

Work activity:
- job hunting
- specialist skill acquisition
- team work.

Family:
- time with family
- holidays
- common interests with partner.

Leisure:
- sport
- pastimes
- hobbies.

There are several methods that you can use to establish your own key areas.

a Bottom up

List all the activities you can think of that you do every day. Divide these into coherent groups. Give each group a title, each title being a key area.

b Top down

Identify the overriding goals in your work and leisure. Decide what main areas you have to concentrate on in order to achieve these goals. These are your key areas.

c Middle out

Consider what would happen if the framework of your life was to disappear, for example, the course you are on no longer exists or you find yourself separated from your family or partner. Identify which main areas would suffer. These are then your key areas.

You can use one method to corroborate the key areas defined by another method.

 Activity 4.2

Now try to establish your key areas. Specify up to nine and make a record of them following the form on page 24. Give each area a title and provide a brief outline if appropriate.

The order does not reflect priority. All key areas are important in achieving your goals.

---

5 Time allocation

Your key resource, time, is limited. You must allocate it to the activities which you have identified as being important in realising your personal goals. It is important that you regularly review how effective you are in using your time. It is equally important that you plan how you are going to use your time in the future.

Activities

Now that you have defined your key areas, you need to identify the activities which have to be performed in each area. You need to decide on the level of detail you require and then list the activities for each key area. There are three time-dependent types of activity:

- **one off**: those occurring once only;
- **ad hoc recurring**: those that occur more than once but the time of occurrence is irregular;
- **regular**: those that recur at the same time each day/week/month.

Listing all activities and categorising them will help you to devise a personal plan.

 Activity 5.1

Copy out a longer version of the form on page 24. List the activities that you have to undertake in two of the key areas you have just defined. Do not go into too much detail or you will lose sight of your objective.

Categorise each activity as one-off, ad hoc recurring or regular.

Consider what you are trying to achieve with each activity.

Analysis of time

You should now realise that if you are to address each key area effectively, you will need to undertake many activities. Do you think this is possible? Have you enough time? You probably think not. Now is a good time to analyse how effective you are in using your time.

It is probably worth starting the next activity at the beginning of a 'normal' week which does not include such things as bank holidays.

Activity 5.2

This exercise is in two parts: time recording and time analysis.

a Time recording

For the next seven days you are to record exactly what you do during each day. Make forms similar to the one on page 25 for each day of the week. On these you should record:
- the time, in minutes, spent on each activity;
- key words describing the activity;
- which key area, if any, the activity is associated with;
- the value you place on the activity, rated as 0 for no value to 5 for highest value;
- any ideas for improving your effectiveness.

b Time analysis

At the end of the week total up the time you spent on each key area and the time you spent on each priority category. Calculate the following percentages:
- percentage time spent on each key area;
- percentage time spent on non-key area activity;
- percentage time spent on high priority (4 or 5) activities;
- percentage time spent on medium priority (2 or 3) activities;
- percentage time spent on low priority (0 or 1) activities.

The time you spend on non-key activity or low priority activities is wasted time. Think how you might eliminate such activities. If you can, then you will have more time available for the important things in life, both work and leisure.

Obstacles revisited

As you have found out, there are many obstacles which can make it difficult to undertake your list of important activities. These obstacles fall into three groups. There are those relating to your own make-up, called psychological obstacles, which affect your attitude and motivation. There are those relating to your type of study. These will affect the daily plans you have made. Finally, there are those relating to your surroundings, called physical obstacles, which limit the effectiveness of your actions. Some examples of these obstacles are as follows.

a Psychological obstacles:

- lack of motivation;

- poor powers of concentration;
- indecision;
- lack of self-discipline;
- inability to complete jobs.

b Study-related obstacles:

- involvement in too many activities;
- too much irrelevant work;
- ineffective reading;
- rush, unplanned activities.

c Physical obstacles:

- noisy living accommodation;
- restricted library opening hours;
- uncomfortable lecture theatres and tutorial rooms.

By careful analysis you should be able to identify the obstacles that are causing you to waste time.

The *psychological obstacles* can only be overcome by understanding your strengths and weaknesses. You have tried to do this in Activity 3.1 and Activity 3.2.

Study-related obstacles can be overcome with practice and self-control. For example, you can learn to read more effectively and more quickly, a skill which will be invaluable for the rest of your life.

Physical obstacles can be overcome by finding a place where you can work effectively. You are likely to find an area with a table and chair, fresh air, warmth and minimal distraction more convivial than trying to work in the middle of a busy student refectory with the blare of heavy metal music and the din of computer games providing the rustic (or perhaps rusty) background!

Plans

It is often the case that the more important something is, the less likely it is urgent and that the more urgent something is, the less likely it is to be important. The coursework due this week may be urgent because you have been putting it off for so long, but is it as important as learning how to organise yourself more effectively in the long term? By adopting a planning strategy which covers both the long term and the short term you should be able to make more effective use of your time.

Activity 5.3

- Try to develop an overall long-term plan for the next 12 months.
- Focus on the activities which are important for each of your key areas.
- Identify key milestones such as examinations.
- You can use an academic planner to record your plan for the next academic year.

Note: Do not include too much detail on your annual plan. It is meant to be a high-level plan which focuses on your key areas. You can use the columns to block out the approximate time needed for each area. Indicate the important milestones on your plan. This approach will provide you with a visual map of the year ahead and is not intended to be an accurate daily work schedule.

A weekly schedule maps out your regular commitments. This enables you to identify the unscheduled time you have available. Having done this you can then allocate this time on a daily basis to the activities you have listed as important. Plan adequate time for breaks and relaxation. Your daily plan is used to organise each day. Major activities should be highlighted. Schedule in your lectures, tutorials, meetings, appointments and specific jobs. At the beginning of each day review what is to be done and adjust your schedule accordingly. *Do not attempt too much* as you are likely to fail and become demoralised.

Remember: 'No' is the most important word in your time management vocabulary.

6 Time management strategies

In the previous sections you have considered the elements of time management in turn. You are now in a position to become a good time manager. The last thing to consider is an overall strategy. Your strategy will enable you to translate your long-term goals into everyday actions.

 Activity 6.1

In two weeks' time you think you have a problem:

- You have to hand in five assignments in the same week.
- You are playing for the first team the weekend before in a tournament at Carlisle.
- On the Tuesday, you have an interview in Bracknell for a placement with a major conglomerate.

Make notes on how you would manage this situation.

In Activity 1.4 and Activity 3.3 you developed a list of steps to manage time effectively. Would you modify any of these having undertaken subsequent exercises? The following may help you to arrive at a list which is appropriate for you:

- clarify your objectives;
- focus on objectives not activities;
- set one major target each day and achieve it;
- periodically record and analyse how you use your time;
- try to eliminate time wasters;
- plan your time;
- make an action list each day;
- make your first hour productive;
- set time limits for each activity;
- make time to do it right first time;
- eliminate recurring crises;
- include quiet time in your day;
- develop the habit of finishing what you start;
- overcome procrastination;
- make time management a daily habit;
- spend time on the more important activities;
- develop your own philosophy of time.

Your strategy should be built around the following steps:
- define goals and expectations;

- cultivate self-knowledge;
- identify key areas;
- define activities for each key area;
- develop a long-term personal action plan;
- establish a short-term schedule of activities;
- organise time available on a daily basis.

Such a framework will help you to decide what to do next.

This was the key to resolving the problem in Activity 6.1. A typical strategy in this case might have been as follows:

a Consider if all elements are within key areas, if not then discard.
b Identify all other activities to be done in the two-week period together with an estimate of time required.
c Identify non-scheduled time.
d Estimate the time involved in the activities stated in Activity 6.1.
e Decide which activities have priority.
f Taking into account the way you work (see Activities 3.1 and 3.2) and the likely obstacles (Activity 2.2), schedule your priority activities.
g Plan how to undertake activities with less priority albeit over a longer period.

 Activity 6.2

And finally consider Heather's plight in the scenario.

Scenario

Heather Moore had just completed a self-study course on time management. The course had been exactly what she needed. It had given her insight into her time problems and how she should establish goals. She was confident that she would have at least two extra hours available each day once she put her newly acquired skills into practice and, of course, once she had caught up with her assignments.

The weeks went by and Heather became more and more frustrated. She wanted to become a more effective time manager but pressures of her studies prevented her from starting.

'What's wrong with me?' she thought. 'I know the things I'm supposed to do, so why don't I do them? I seem to be my own worst enemy!'

Are you your own worst enemy?

Working through the exercises should have helped you to address your time management weaknesses and thus become more effective in the things you do. Time management is about having the right attitude of mind.

7 Bibliography

Austin, B. (1986) *Making effective use of executive time*, London, Management Update.

Douglass, M.E. and Douglass, D.N. (1980) *Manage your time, manage your work, manage yourself*, New York, Amacon.

Rogerson, S. (1989) *Project skills handbook*, Bromley, Chartwell-Bratt.

8 Activity forms

Key steps in effective time management	Leave this space for later modifications
1	
2	

My outstanding activities	
Activities	Priority

My most important outstanding activities			
Activity	Why is this activity important?	Time	Date
1			

Obstacles that prevent me from achieving		
Obstacle	Why does the obstacle exist?	Priority
1		

My most significant obstacles	
Obstacle	What can I do to overcome the obstacle?
1	

My key areas	
Title	Brief outline
1	

The key activities I have to do		
Activity	Category	Key area

Time recording Monday

Time	No. mins	Activity	Key area (if any)	Priority 0–5	Idea for improvement
0700					
0800					
0900					
1000					
1100					
1200					
1300					
1400					
1500					
1600					
1700					
1800					
1900					
2000					
2100					
2200					
2300					

Part B: Managing your learning

Introduction

The context of higher education is changing as a greater proportion of the population is able to benefit from a university experience. As a consequence, the methods of teaching, learning and assessment are being adapted to accommodate a larger and more diverse student population.

As a student you may be full- or part-time, study during the day or evening, be on the university premises or study through distance-learning packages. You are likely to experience learning in a wide range of contexts, including large lectures, seminars, workshops and laboratory work. While these may be familiar, the scale may be different; for example, lectures with over two hundred students are now common. Likewise, group work is becoming more popular as a teaching technique as it has many recognised benefits to the learner which tend not to be found in more traditional methods. The impact of new technologies is also likely to change your experience as a learner. For instance, you may come across video conferencing and interactive computer programmes as these become more widespread.

In addition there is now a recognition that traditional unseen examinations are only one form of assessment, and that you will benefit by being assessed in a range of ways which will develop more skills and abilities. This might include assessed course work or research projects, your contribution to a group project, multiple-choice questions, presentation skills and seen examination papers. This growing range of assessment formats may require more strategic organisation on your part.

As a learner you need to recognise and play to your strengths and improve your weaknesses. You will be able to do this more effectively if you recognise your preferred learning style and capitalise upon it. This part of the book has been designed to help you do this.

Objectives

At the end of this part you should be able to:
  a identify the different contexts in which learning may take place;
  b analyse your strengths and weaknesses as a learner;
  c develop strategies to make you a more effective learner in different contexts.

9   Contexts of teaching and learning

Introduction to the range of teaching and learning opportunities

As a student you will be taught and you will learn in a variety of different contexts. Some of these will be necessary to achieve specific learning outcomes, eg laboratories to carry out practical experiments; others are more useful for meeting the needs of your personal development, eg tutorials.

The range of teaching and learning contexts is wide. You may experience only a few of them and you may spend more time in one context than another.

 Activity 9.1

From the list below tick those that you regularly participate in:

- [ ] lecture
- [ ] seminar (groups of more than twelve)
- [ ] tutorial (groups of under five)
- [ ] individual tutorial
- [ ] workshop
- [ ] laboratory
- [ ] supervised project work
- [ ] open-learning materials
- [ ] computer-aided studying
- [ ] library research
- [ ] group work
- [ ] other

Make a note of those that you are unfamiliar with and read on to learn more about them.

Teaching and learning contexts

Lecture

A lecture is recognised traditionally as an address to a large number of students which takes place in a lecture theatre, often with raked seating. Usually the lecturer speaks directly to the students for a large percentage of the time while they take notes. The lecturer may use the lecture to raise students' awareness of conceptual issues rather than to transmit information that can be conveyed through handouts and reference material. There may be some interaction if the lecturer encourages questions or organises mini activities that can be carried out without much movement.

Seminar

A seminar gives you the opportunity to meet in smaller groups, usually with 12 to 20 participants. The focus of the seminar can be the topic of a recent lecture, the subject of previous reading or research, or an activity devised by the tutor to develop knowledge and skills that you may not be introduced to in another context. It should be participative; you may be asked to present a topic, join a group discussion, work through practical problems or take part in a more interactive session such as role play.

Tutorial

Tutorials with about five students are less common now in higher education. They do give you the opportunity, however, to be part of a small, cohesive group that is likely to offer mutual support to each member. The topic of the tutorial may be similar to that of the seminar, but there is more opportunity for deeper discussion and interaction with the lecturer.

Individual tutorial

This is often used to discuss pieces of work such as essays or to monitor the progress of a dissertation or project. You should take this opportunity to discuss your academic interests or problems.

Workshop

A workshop is an interactive learning context with a much greater emphasis on activity than in a seminar. It may take the place of a lecture/seminar because it offers more time to discuss topics and enables students to explore concepts more fully with a lecturer.

Laboratory

When working in a laboratory the emphasis will be on practical work. Often you will be asked to watch a demonstration and then to replicate the procedure. You may work alone or in pairs or small groups, however the total number of students in the laboratory is unlikely to be very large. Laboratory work can take various forms, but you are likely to be engaged in active experimental work: observing, testing and recording results.

Supervised project work

The emphasis so far has been on quite controlled teaching and learning contexts. There are others which will give you much greater freedom to define your area of learning and the method by which you learn. Project work can be one such context. The variables may include:

- the topic, which may be set by or negotiated with the lecturer;
- working alone or in a group;
- the time span, which may cover a weekly allowance over a semester or year or be condensed into a short concentrated period of a week or fortnight;
- possibly a 'learning contract' stating your aims and objectives and a timetable of planned work.

Open-learning materials

These take the form of materials either published professionally or produced by lecturers for specific purposes. They give information in the form of facts, theories and considered opinions and assist you in analysing and evaluating them through set activities. They give you the opportunity to work at your own pace, setting your own timetable of learning. This book is an example of open-learning material.

Computer-aided learning

Many of the characteristics of open learning apply to computer-aided studying. This form of learning can offer greater diversity because of the possibility of storing information in a vast computer memory. Hypermedia packages allow you to choose to follow up areas of your own particular interest rather than follow a designated route. Some programmes are interactive and pose questions to the user as well as correcting answers.

Library research

To build upon the knowledge you gain in your interaction with lecturers and other students in lectures and seminars you will need to research information in a library. Usually this is done individually. Libraries provide a wider source of information to draw upon: historical, geographical, ideological and so on. For more information on library use see your university or college libraries.

Group work

Your ability to learn may be enhanced by working in a group. This context of teaching and learning is becoming increasingly common in higher education. Group work allows you to pool knowledge and skills in order to provide you with the benefits of a greater depth of synthesis of ideas. Working in a group will also help you develop a range of valuable personal skills. The method of group work may vary. You may be assigned to a group or the group may be self-selected.

As you progress through your course you may be asked to choose between courses that will require you to learn in different ways. It is useful to be aware of what will be expected of you in each context and to recognise that you may do better in some contexts than in others. Getting to know more about the variety of teaching and learning methods used at university will therefore help you make reasoned decisions and, as a result, perform more effectively.

What learning experiences can you expect from different contexts?

You have seen that there is a wide variety of teaching and learning contexts in which you will probably participate while you are studying. The way that you learn will be different in each of them. If you can be aware of the methods by which you are taught and learn you will be better prepared for the demands made upon you in different circumstances and therefore should learn more easily and effectively.

The next activity is designed to help you to identify the types of learning experiences you most commonly participate in.

 Activity 9.2

Below is a list of descriptive words that can be applied to teaching and learning contexts. Write down the forms of teaching/learning that you most associate with it from the list in Activity 9.1.

- active
- passive
- self-directed
- lecturer led
- information gathering
- analytical
- evaluative
- creative.

If your experience is typical of traditional methods of teaching and learning you probably equated *active* with project work and group work and *passive* with lectures. The situation, however, is more complex than this and it will help to consider what these terms actually mean.

Active learning involves you, the learner, as a participant in the learning process. It is not controlled solely by the lecturer and you take responsibility for your own learning. You are likely to be engaged in the learning process through:

- linking concepts and ideas together;
- applying concepts in new situations;
- relating materials together in new ways;
- problem solving;
- restructuring knowledge for different contexts;
- synthesising material, ie bringing ideas together from different sources;
- analysing information by trying to find explanations for phenomena;
- defining the aims and the pace of learning.

Passive learning occurs when you are on the receiving end of the learning process. Your experiences are less engaged and more repetitive. You are likely to:

- record and regurgitate knowledge and ideas;
- replicate ideas and concepts given to you by others;
- reproduce material uncritically;
- memorise material, sometimes with only limited understanding;
- have little control over the forms and pace of the material covered.

Lectures can be quite *active* if you are making links with other learning experiences – especially if you are not just writing down every word in the hope that it will mean something later! It depends on your involvement with the material. Some situations can be a mixture, eg seminars may be led and controlled by a lecturer, but you may be required to take an *active* part. Similarly, computer-aided learning is *passive* in that you sit at a keyboard and probably don't move around very much. However, you are *active* in the sense of making decisions such as when to start and stop, and you may be engaged in complex, problem-solving activities.

It is important to recognise that different contexts will require you to take differing levels of responsibility for managing your own learning.

10 What sort of learner are you?

How we learn

Early theories of how we learn tended to emphasise changed behaviour as evidence of learning having taken place. To achieve this change, it was assumed that conditioning, a system of rewards and punishments, was fundamental to the process of learning. Furthermore, conditioning requires reinforcement to motivate the learned behaviour. In the classic behavioural laboratory model, animals were often used to demonstrate this process of learning. For example, if an animal presses a lever that produces food, the reinforcement of getting food is likely to encourage the animal to repeat the behaviour. In education, praise or good grades can reinforce acceptable behaviour in a student. This theory of learning stresses the role of the teacher in devising the patterns of conditioning and reinforcement. The student has little involvement in developing the learning programme.

However, by contrast, present theories of learning stress the importance of the role of the learner in the learning process. Such theories emphasise the active role of the learner and how this involves a negotiating interaction between student and lecturer to arrive at an experience which matches the needs of the student to the aims of the course he or she is studying.

The educational researcher Kolb (1984) suggests that we learn more effectively by being actively involved in learning. His model (Figure 10.1) starts with an active, concrete experience rather than the more passive method of being taught theory first and then applying it.

Kolb's model is based on a cycle which includes both active and passive learning and provides both concrete and abstract experience. It proceeds through four stages:

a **Concrete experience**: you do something.

b **Observation and reflection**: you consider what happened.

c **Formation of abstract concepts and generalisations**: you draw on your consideration to form concepts and generalisations.

d **Testing implications of concepts in new situations:** you develop a hypothesis and test it out, which leads to a new experience.

This cycle can then be repeated as a spiral, on-going model, constantly learning from new experiences and modifying concepts to test in new situations.

Figure 10.1: Kolb's learning cycle

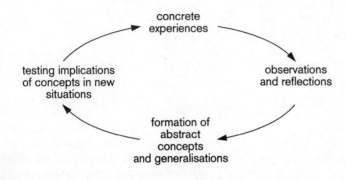

 Activity 10.1

Give an example of a learning experience which you feel depended on the conditioning method of learning. You may be able to look back and remember learning by rote, eg your multiplication tables or a poem for a concert as a child. The rewards might have been praise, a gold star, or applause to encourage you to perform well next time.

Give an example of a learning experience which you feel depended on the active method of learning.

Looking back on these experiences, which do you feel led to deeper, longer-lasting or more effective learning and why?

What is your preferred learning style?

The previous discussion of learning theory shows that there are many ways in which we can learn. But do we all learn in the same way? It has been suggested that although there are different methods of learning we each actually prefer to learn in a way particular to ourselves. This may be due to a variety of personal, social or cultural reasons. Knowing that you prefer to learn in a particular way can help you choose courses which suit you best.

Kolb has devised a *learning styles inventory* which indicates the preferred style of the respondent, though this can change over time and in different situations. The inventory asks the learner to rank in order four descriptions of themselves. The four descriptions match four learning styles which are also related to Kolb's model of the learning process (see Figure 10.1). The four styles are:

CE concrete experience
RO reflective observation
AC abstract conceptualisation
AE active experimentation.

Although Kolb stresses the importance of the learner moving through the learning cycle, he recognises that different people will have their own needs and goals and will therefore emphasise one part of the learning cycle over others; in other words, they will have a preference for one or more learning styles.

The inventory helps the learner identify her/his preferred style. No one style is better than another. It is more important to be able to use each when appropriate. Armed with this knowledge it is then possible to try to redress when you either overemphasise or avoid certain styles so that you can create a more balanced approach to learning. For example, if you prefer active experimentation you may not have spent enough time reflecting on what you have done and this could lead you to miss interesting observations that might be useful in developing your work further.

To find out what sort of learner you are, compare your descriptions of yourself to those suggested by the learning styles inventory. The inventory identifies learners who prefer:

- **concrete experience** as people who would describe themselves as 'receptive, feeling, accepting, intuitive, present-orientated';

- **reflective observation** as people who would describe themselves as 'tentative, watching, observing, reflecting, reserved';

- **abstract conceptualisation** as people who would describe themselves as 'analytical, thinking, evaluative, logical, rational';

- **active experimentation** as people who would describe themselves as: 'practical, doing, active, pragmatic, responsible'.

(Quotations adapted from Kolb, 1984, page 27.)

The following paragraphs give a fuller description of how your learning style may influence the way you prefer to learn.

An *orientation toward concrete experience* focuses on being involved in experiences and dealing with immediate human situations in a personal way. It emphasises feeling as opposed to thinking, a concern with the uniqueness and complexity of present reality as opposed to theories and generalisations, an intuitive, 'artistic' approach as opposed to the systematic, scientific approach to problems. People with a concrete experience orientation enjoy and are good at relating to others. They are often good intuitive decision makers and function well in unstructured situations. People with this orientation value relating to people, being involved in real situations, and an open-minded approach to life.

An *orientation toward reflective observation* focuses on understanding the meaning of ideas and situations by carefully observing and impartially describing them. It emphasises understanding as opposed to practical application, a concern with what is true or how things happen as opposed to what is practical, an emphasis on reflection as opposed to action. People with a reflective orientation enjoy thinking about the meaning of situations and ideas and are good at seeing their implications. They are good at looking at things from different perspectives and at appreciating different points of view. They like to rely on their own thoughts and feelings to form opinions. People with this orientation value patience, impartiality and considered, thoughtful judgement.

An *orientation toward abstract conceptualisation* focuses on using logic, ideas, and concepts. It emphasises thinking as opposed to feeling, a concern with building general theories as opposed to intuitively understanding unique, specific areas, a scientific as opposed to an artistic approach to problems. A person with an abstract conceptual orientation enjoys and is good at systematic planning, manipulation of abstract symbols and quantitative analysis. People with this orientation value precision, the rigour and discipline of analysing ideas, and the aesthetic quality of a neat, conceptual system.

An *orientation toward active experimentation* focuses on actively influencing people and changing situations. It emphasises practical applications as opposed to reflective understanding, a pragmatic concern with what works as opposed to what is absolute truth, an emphasis on doing as opposed to observing. People with an active experimentation orientation enjoy and are good at getting things accomplished. They are willing to take some risk to achieve their objectives. They also value having an impact and influence on the environment around them and like to see results.

(Kolb, 1984, pages 34–5.)

You may feel that your learning style is, in fact, a combination of these categories. That is quite common. However, you will be likely to show a preference for abstractness or concreteness, and action or reflection. Now that you have a clearer understanding of your preferred learning style you may like to reflect on your typical learning contexts and see if your abilities to learn in them may be explained by either a compatibility or incompatibility between the teaching style and your preferred learning style.

The implications of your learning style

 Activity 10.2

Now you are going to do a *SWOT* analysis. SWOT stands for *strengths, weaknesses, opportunities* and *threats*. Completing the SWOT chart will enable you to look at these four areas in relation to your preferred learning style. This should lead you to be aware of the implications of your particular SWOT for your programme of study. For example, if you prefer *active experimentation* you will achieve more in situations when you are asked to generate and apply new ideas. On the other hand, you may find it difficult and frustrating to repeat activities or perhaps to appraise the viability of your ideas.

Copy out the SWOT chart below and begin by filling in your preferred style at the top of the sheet. Under each heading of strengths, weaknesses, opportunities and threats, make a note of the examples that fit your learning style. The example has been started for you to follow:

Preferred learning style: active experimentation

strengths	**weaknesses**
tend to lead group work	
opportunities	**threats**

Maximise your strengths and work on your weaknesses – how to do it better!

 Activity 10.3

When you have completed the SWOT analysis consider how you might develop your strengths, make use of your opportunities, improve your weaknesses and control the threats. Redraw the SWOT chart and insert new headings:

develop strengths	**improve weaknesses**
make use of opportunities	**control threats**

Activity 10.4

Look at the choice of courses/modules on offer to you on your study programme for the next semester or year.

Find out what their methods of teaching and learning are, eg lectures or self-supported study. Make a list of them.

a Consider which courses require you to draw on your particular strengths. How might you develop your strengths in this area to turn them into opportunities?

b Consider which courses/modules reveal your weaknesses. How might you improve your weaknesses in this area so that they are not a threat?

c How might your preferred learning style affect other areas of studying, eg time management? How might you turn these into opportunities?

11 Strategies for more effective learning

Deep and surface learning

Recent research has distinguished between *deep* and *surface* approaches to learning.
Read through the following passage.

Bonding to new rights and roles for students

Now that patients and rail travellers have charters, it is time that students got one too.
Individual colleges have been experimenting for some time now with some form of
student contract, but these have mainly been about the quality of facilities and
services. What we need is nothing less than a sort of government bond, cashable by
students at a place and a time which suits them best. The training vouchers for 16-
to 19-year-olds being piloted give some clue about how a scheme might work, but
they are still far too restricted, because the real problems are those of mature would-
be students.

We have got used to the pattern of higher education: an entitlement to payment of
fees and to an award subject to means test. As long, that is, as you want a full-time
degree course. You are not, of course, entitled to the personal circumstances which
enable you to take up your opportunity. You may be unable to do so for any one of
several reasons which have nothing to do with your ability to succeed. Even that sort
of partial entitlement does not extend to full-time sub-degree work or to part-time
study of any kind. This is plainly discriminatory. Why should individuals who are not
ready to tackle a degree because they were unable or unwilling to stay on at 16 be
disadvantaged when they want to come back, after 19? Is it punishment for being too
poor, too foolish or too bored to continue?

Some enlightened education authorities, those grievously maligned bodies, recognised the inequity and provided discretionary awards for mature students taking up
full-time courses in further education. Now they have nearly all stopped doing so.
Fears of charge-capping no doubt have a lot to do with it, perhaps also an unwilling-
ness to put money into colleges which are heading for corporate quasi-independ-
ence. The LEAs were enlightened not just because they could see the personal, social
benefits to the recipients of awards, but because they were doing something to
improve the national stock of well-educated, well-trained people. Without this kind
of support our scandalous and disastrous waste of undeveloped ability will go on, and
our national industrial and commercial performance will continue to be poor. At the
moment we cry out against skill shortages and simultaneously deny ourselves one of
the best means of correcting them.

So, why not a student charter? Perhaps the problems are those of definition:
entitlement to how much of what? Work needs to be done on this, or we may find that

for fear of funding flower arrangers we shut out engineers and computer programmers. But if it is right, as it must be, to support people through five years of post-compulsory education, full-time from 16 to 21, ending with a degree, it should be possible to find a formula which offered the equivalent to those who start later, attend less regularly, or pursue a wider range of qualifications.

Michael Austin, *TES*, 19 March 1993.

 Activity 11.1

Having read through the article, try to answer the following questions *without* looking back at it.

a Jot down quickly the main points of the article you have just read. Who wrote it?

b Summarise the writer's main arguments.

c Suggest arguments for and against the student charter proposed by the writer and suggest alternative models for the 1990s.

How far did you get? Did you find **a** easier than **c**? If so, what made **c** more difficult?

 Activity 11.2

Look at your answers to Activity 11.1 again and then score them on the grid below (adapted from Entwistle and Entwistle, 1991).

Circle a score at one point of the scale. Did you?

Understand the material for yourself	③②①⓪①②③	Simply reproduce parts of the content
Interact critically with the content	③②①⓪①②③	Accept ideas and information passively
Relate ideas to previous assessment knowledge and experience	③②①⓪①②③	Concentrate only on requirements
Use organising principles to integrate ideas	③②①⓪①②③	Not reflect on purposes or strategies
Relate evidence to conclusions	③②①⓪①②③	Memorise facts and procedures routinely

Examine the logic of the argument	③②①⓪①②③	Fail to distinguish guiding principles or patterns
If you were scoring high marks at this end of the scale you are presently engaging in a deep approach to learning		If you were scoring high marks at this end of the scale you are engaging in a surface approach to learning

You may have noticed that:
- question **a** required a regurgitation of the main points;
- question **b** demanded more understanding of the arguments;
- question **c** expected you to debate the ideas and suggest new ones – enabling you to engage more fully with the subject matter.

There was a move from *surface* to *deep* learning in the progression of the demands.

You are more likely to score highly on the *deep* approach to learning if you:
- are motivated to understand the topic;
- already have a good knowledge base;
- are active in your learning;
- engage in learning with others;
- have planned, experienced, reflected and applied the new learning experience (see Kolb's cycle, Chapter 10, pages 32–3).

By contrast you are more likely to be involved at a *surface* level if you:
- have little interest in the topic;
- had no prior knowledge of the subject matter;
- had limited opportunity to discuss it with others;
- had no chance to plan, experience, reflect or apply your new learning experience (ie experience Kolb's learning cycle, see Chapter 10, pages 32–3 again);
- are passive in your learning.

You may need to reflect on these points in the light of the learning process you have just undertaken.

The more you are engaged in a deep approach, the more likely it is that you will be able to:
- use what you have learned in the future;
- transfer and apply your skills to new areas;
- develop critical analyses of ideas and information;
- assimilate new knowledge into an existing framework.

Clearly this activity is only a starting point for you to reflect on your approach to learning. You might find it useful to go back to Activity 11.2 and score it again for your approach to learning on parts of your current course. If you are scoring towards the surface end you may want to consider how to move towards the deep approach which will make you a more effective learner.

In Chapter 9, pages 30–1, we considered the characteristics of *active* and *passive* learning. By linking this with concepts of *surface* and *deep* learning you will see that you are more likely to become engaged in deep learning if you become more active in the learning environment.

One way to do this is to ensure that you participate more fully in the learning process, even where you may feel that you have little control. The following sections, which focus on *networking* and *becoming an active learner*, may help you start to deal with this.

Networking

One way of trying to improve your learning approach is to form study networks with other students on your course.

> *'Study networks are a form of self-help group for students.'*
> (Hartley, 1992, page 26.)

Networks go beyond a particular task and provide additional support to that which is given by your tutors.

Why form study networks?

Study networks provide opportunities for you to:
- be a more active learner;
- share resources;
- pool ideas;
- tackle problems;
- teach as well as learn as members of a network/group;
- catch up on missed work;
- discuss and explore topics beyond formal sessions;
- get to know more students;
- develop confidence;
- share tasks.

How can you set up study networks?

If these do not emerge out of the context of your course you may need to do something to help generate them.

You could consider the following:
- ask your tutor for help in setting them up;
- suggest that your student representatives call a meeting;
- call a meeting yourself or with a group of friends.

What happens next?
- explain the purpose of the group (as above);
- split into small groups if necessary;
- decide when, where and how regularly you will meet;
- agree an early date for the next meeting to maintain momentum;
- decide how you will keep in touch, eg exchange telephone numbers or use notice-boards.

Some of the hints in Part C: Working in groups and Part D: Managing your group project may be helpful here. Study networks are more informal and do not always centre on a task, but some of the rules on group management apply.

Becoming a more active learner

Some activities, such as practical laboratory work, are already active. Others will vary. This section will try to show you how to develop strategies to increase your involvement in the learning process.

Formal lectures

Formal lectures can be a very passive experience for students. It is always tempting – but not very easy – to try to scribble down everything that is said, and the results can be indecipherable or not comprehensive.

Lectures are mostly used for:
- giving information;
- alerting you to relevant knowledge;
- explaining complex problems and ideas.

Bear in mind Kolb's learning cycle from Chapter 10. You will learn better if you follow through the cycle. Dennison and Kirk (1990) have adapted Kolb's cycle to 'Do, Review, Learn, Apply'. You may find it easier to remember this format.

Figure 11.1

Remember your preferred learning style may mean that you are more comfortable in some aspects of the cycle than others and you may need to compensate by developing your weaker areas.

By following through the cycle you may experience the following:

DO	attend lectures
REVIEW	discuss in tutorials/seminars, use study networks
LEARN	back up with additional reading, relate to other theories and ideas
APPLY	use knowledge and understanding in a new context, eg problem solving, group project, assignment.

If you are not going to write down everything that is being said, what can you do to use lectures effectively?

a Ask if there will be a handout. If so, you could add points to it.
b Listen and try to summarise points, say every ten minutes. You could write up the points more fully after the lecture. This would make you think about them rather than merely regurgitating the ideas.
c Use your study network to develop ideas or fill in points you missed or did not understand.

 Activity 11.3

Identify some of the other problems that you have with formal lectures and suggest how you might deal with them.

Here are some you might have included, with suggestions on how to deal with them:

Problems	Solutions
The OHTs are difficult to read.	Mention this to the lecturer. Ask if you could have copies. Get in early and sit at the front.
You cannot hear at the back.	Let the lecturer know straight away. Move nearer.
You cannot understand what is being taught.	Ask for clarification. Make a note of your point and take it up in your tutorial/seminar. Use your study network. Seek help from the lecturer after the lecture. Suggest a 'Thoughts, Concerns and Questions' box. This is left at the back of the class and students can leave notes for the lecturer at the end of each session to be dealt with at the start of the next (Andreson, 1990). This could be done anonymously. Follow it up in the library.

Tutorials and seminars

Many courses are organised around the large lecture with opportunities for smaller group work in tutorials or seminars. These sessions are likely to range from groups of 8 to 20. They may give you opportunities to discuss lectures or to develop ideas further. Some may be organised around small group work, others will require students to give a seminar paper.

Tutorials or seminars should give you opportunities to be an active learner, but what happens if problems arise to prevent this?

 Activity 11.4

What might stop you getting the most out of your seminar and what can you do about it?

Here are some examples of problems you may experience. What solutions can you suggest?
- I never get a chance to make my points because a few students always dominate the sessions.
- We are always wandering from the point, it is very frustrating.
- Students always arrive late, we waste so much time.

- No one speaks, so it is like having another lecture.
- I'm still not sure what will be required in the exam/course assignments.
- It's difficult to discuss when you can't see all of the students.

Write down any particular problems you have come across.

Here are some suggested solutions to the problems above:

Problems

I never get a chance to make my points, a few students always dominate the sessions.

What can be done?

Try and speak at the start of the session. Research shows if you don't say something early on, you probably won't speak in the session at all. If necessary, prepare it beforehand.

We are always wandering from the point, it's very frustrating.

Ask your tutor if it is worth pursuing this point. There are ways of doing this that will not cause offence: *'I'm not quite sure how this fits in with what we were doing before'* would give your tutor the chance to show you the links you may not have seen ... or move the discussion on!

Students always arrive late, we waste so much time.

Suggest that as a group you establish some ground rules. These could relate to start and finish times, but also to rules for discussion, eg agreement to listen and not interrupt.

No one speaks, so it is like having another lecture.

Prepare questions to ask before you arrive.

Suggest working in groups on tasks.

Suggest the tutor takes up the points from the 'Thoughts, Concerns and Questions' box. These could be covered in tutorials rather than in the lecture.

I'm still not sure what will be required in the exam/course assignments.	Ask for the assessment criteria.
	Suggest you would like to spend some time going through these.
	Ask if you can do some outline answers for discussion.
It's difficult to discuss when you can't see all of the students.	Ask if you can move the furniture so you can see everyone.

Know the rules – matching learning to assessment criteria

On some courses you may get a choice on how you are assessed. On modular courses there may be a variety of assessment approaches and you may be able to choose some courses with the assessment pattern in mind.

 Activity 11.5

What types of assessment exist on your course? Write down as many as you can.

Here are some examples:

Written work
- course work assignments
- unseen examinations
- seen examinations
- multiple-choice tests
- time-constrained assignments
- laboratory reports
- reporting on group assignments.

Audio-visual work
- video/audio materials
- painting and drawing
- posters.

Practical assessment
- performance
- group presentations

- experiments
- projects
- contribution to seminars
- practical problem solving.

 Activity 11.6

Identify those types of assessment which you are likely to face and note their advantages (pluses) and disadvantages (minuses) for you. Look back at your preferred learning style. You may find that some aspects will affect your success in assessment. For example, if you are an *active experimenter* you may be better at practical assessment. If you are better at *abstract conceptualisation* you may prefer examinations. There are, of course, other factors involved.

Although you may get some choice, most people have to tackle assessment they do not like. Consider how you might turn your minuses into pluses. For example, if you do not like exams try to identify the reasons and some possible solutions, such as:

I don't do well in exams because ... I get too nervous.
Did you plan your revision early enough?
Did you practise with past papers?
Did you take deep breaths to calm you down?

Whatever form of assessment you are undertaking, you should be clear about what is being assessed, ie the criteria that will be used when your work is marked. Ask your tutor if you are not clear about this.

 Activity 11.7

Identify other types of assessment you want to improve. Ask tutors, friends and use study networks to help you with this.

Managing your time effectively

Effective time management is crucial if you are to make the most of your opportunities as an undergraduate. This section provides an introduction, but you should also read Part A: Time management.

You may be busy, but are you effective as a learner?

To be more effective you need to:
- know yourself as a learner;
- know how you spend your time now;
- plan your programme.

Know yourself as a learner

Activity 11.8

Answer the following questions using the symbols below:

😊 agree   😐 don't know   🙁 disagree

a I work best at the following times:
- ◯ morning
- ◯ afternoon
- ◯ evening
- ◯ night

Are you working at your best time *now*? If not, *change*.

b The tasks I tackle first each day are:
- ◯ the easiest
- ◯ the most difficult
- ◯ the ones on top of the pile
- ◯ the ones all of my friends are doing

If you are avoiding things, do you miss deadlines? Do you hand in work that is not up to scratch?

c I prefer to:
- ◯ work fast and then correct
- ◯ work slowly and get it right first time
- ◯ attack the whole task
- ◯ tackle it in small chunks without an overall plan
- ◯ be easily distracted
- ◯ plan out a strategy and stick to it

Does your approach work for you – or do you need another way of doing things?

d Where do you work best?

◯   in your room
◯   in the university library
◯   in other university rooms
◯   in the park
◯   other (write in)

Look back at the answers you have given and check that when, where and how you work is helping you to study effectively.

If not, change your learning habits *now*!

Know how you spend your time now

 Activity 11.9

The best way to assess how your time is spent is to keep a time log for a few days. Make your own log using the headings given below and try it out.

day	activity	start	finish	duration	comment
Mon.	lecture	10	11	1hr	useful
	coffee bar	11	12.45	1.45hr	too long

 Activity 11.10

At the end of the few days, work out how much of your time was spent:
- learning...............hrs
- sleeping...............hrs
- in recreation...............hrs
- working for money...............hrs
- surviving, ie shopping, cooking, etc...............hrs

Was this the right balance for you? If not, think about how you might be able to change it.

Plan your programme

You need to be able to manage your time so that you meet your deadlines. Make sure you:
- check what needs to be done now;
- establish your priorities;
- put your energies into achieving them.

 Activity 11.11

Make a list of all the pieces of work which you need to do before the end of the term/semester. The following example may help you.

Task 1
Group project to be completed in two parts. Presentation by 10 June. Report by 17 June (2,000 words)

Task 2
Two-hour examination on 11 June

Task 3
Three-hour examination on 12 June

Task 4
Course assignment on 21 June (2,500 words)

Task 5
One-hour multiple-choice paper on 24 May

Task 6
A short report (1,000 words) and individual seminar paper (30mins) on 6 May

It is now mid-April...

Now identify the tasks that you need to complete this term/semester.

 Activity 11.12

In order to prioritise, you need to identify what is involved in each task and what the deadlines are for each component. You may find it helpful to use an academic planner, referred to in Chapter 5, to keep track of this. You also need to decide which are the most important activities – perhaps some carry more marks or weightings than others. The example below uses Tasks 4 and 5 of Activity 11.11.

activity		timescale		
task involved	what is needed	deadline	time	comments
Essay (Task 4)	2,500 words	21 May hand in	5 weeks left	should start earlier next time
	word processor	16–20 May	5 days	are machines available then?
	library	now mid-April	depends if books are in	order earlier next time
	attend lectures	21 April— 2 May		should give basics
	collect handouts	21 April— 2 May		useful as a guide
multiple-choice exam (Task 5)	one hour exam (revision only counts for 10%)	24 May take exam	5 weeks	spend one hour per week until exam

 Activity 11.13

Now outline your own tasks in the same way, using the same headings.

 Activity 11.14

This final activity will show you how to plot your tasks on a timescale, again using the tasks identified in Activity 11.11. Now draw your own blank timescale and plot your tasks.

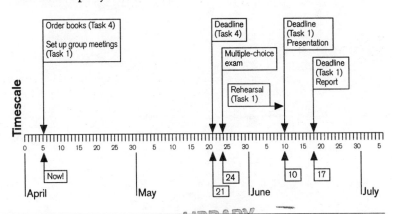

12 Summary

This part aimed to give you some strategies for managing your learning more effectively. It has given you an opportunity to consider the range of contexts in which learning occurs and has provided some frameworks in which you can reflect on your own preferences as a learner. Current research indicates that you learn more effectively if you are active in your learning and can learn in a deep way. This moves you beyond the superficial and enables you to apply what you have learned in different contexts.

You will be a more effective learner if you can control your learning environment. This might mean being more involved in lectures or setting up study networks to provide additional support from among your peers. Performing well in your assessment is crucial. You may have some choice in the assessment options, particularly on modular courses, but you may not. In this case you need to be aware of your weaknesses and try to develop strategies to overcome them. This is the key to managing your learning overall – build on your strengths and try to overcome your weaknesses!

13 Bibliography

Andreson, L. (1990) *Lecturing to large groups*, Birmingham, SCED.

Atkins, M. J. *et al.* (1993) *Assessment issues in higher education*, Employment Department, Further and Higher.

Austin, M. (1993) Bonding to new rights and roles for students, *Times Higher Education Supplement*, No.1063, 19 March, p 14.

Dennison, B. and Kirk, R. (1990) *Do, review, learn, apply: a simple guide to experiential learning*, Oxford, Basil Blackwell.

Entwistle, N. (1992) *The impact of teaching on learning outcomes in higher education*, Sheffield, CVCP.

Entwistle, N. J. and Entwistle, A. C. (1991) *Developing, revising and examining conceptual understanding: the student experience and its implications*, University of Edinburgh, Centre for Research on Learning and Instruction.

Hartley, J. (1992), Supporting student learning on a part-time course, in Gibbs, G. (ed.), *Improving the quality of student learning*, Bristol, Technical and Educational Services.

Kolb, D. A. *et al.* (1984) *Organisational psychology*, 4th ed., London.

Part C: Working in groups

Introduction

We will now focus in more detail on group work. The aim of this part is to develop your skills in group work.

Objectives

When you have read through and completed the exercises in this part you should be able to:
- consider the research evidence which underpins group activity;
- recognise characteristics of effective and ineffective groups;
- understand the processes involved in group formation.

You may use this part as an individual student or as a group that is planning a project. Both individual and group activities are included for you to try. To develop further your skills in project work you should also read Part D: Managing your group project.

14 Why work in groups?

Current context of higher education

You may have been asked to work with other students in a group formation already. If you have not, you may well be before the end of your course. Current methods of teaching and learning are laying a greater emphasis on students participating in more active learning situations, rather than attending traditional passive lectures.

What is a group?

Activity 14.1

We all belong to groups. Try to list some groups that you do, or did, belong to. The suggestions below will start you off:
- family
- sports team

You have probably listed a wide variety of groups. What makes them 'groups'? The *Concise Oxford Dictionary* defines a group as:

'number of persons or things belonging or classed together or forming a whole'. (Sykes, 1976, page 474.)

Some psychologists suggest that there also needs to be interaction between members and a perception of themselves as a group. Look at your list of groups – would you agree with these definitions?

Psychologists divide groups into 'primary' and 'secondary' types. Primary groups are those made up of small numbers of people who are in regular contact; secondary groups are made up of large numbers where participants are unlikely to know all the members. This study guide is concerned with *primary* groups.

Activity 14.2

Primary groups share a number of common characteristics. Can you name any of them?

Some of the characteristics that you have suggested may also be present in the types of groups we belong to that are based on social interaction or working practices. We will address work-based groups here as this most suits the type of groups you will be working in at university. Adair (1989, page 6) defines the characteristics of these types of groups as follows:

- a definable membership – a collection of two or more people identifiable by name or type;
- group consciousness – the members think of themselves as a group, have a collective perception of unity, a conscious identification with each other;
- a sense of shared purpose – the members have the same common task or goals or interests;
- interdependence – the members need the help of one another to accomplish the purposes for which they joined the group;
- interaction – the members communicate with one another, influence one another, react to one another;
- ability to act in a unitary manner – the group can work as a single organism.

So far we have discussed groups. However, there is also the related term 'team' that we should consider. A team is a group which works together in a combined effort. This definition owes much to the use of 'team' to describe horses or oxen harnessed together to pull carts and farm equipment. You may feel that the group work that you are asked to participate in at university requires the more task-orientated and outcome-specific activity associated with teams. There is, however, an overlap between the meanings of team and group. In our context the term *group* includes the notion of *team*.

Advantages of working in a group

Developing competent working practices

a Efficiency
It can be more efficient to work as a group. Early research into industrial relations by Mayo at the Hawthorne Plant, Chicago (1927–32) suggested that group work boosts levels of productivity. The research programme segregated a group of women and monitored their behaviour as their working conditions were changed. Their productivity continued to improve. Mayo concluded that this was due to the benefits of working as a cohesive group. By being separated, the women developed their own codes of values, rules and practices and gained a higher satisfaction by controlling the pace of their work.

b Effectiveness
Group work is an important strategy for effective working practices in organisations. It is more useful to put together temporary groups to tackle specific tasks. In this way groups can be made up of those people who have the necessary skills for the particular activity. At its completion the group can be dispersed and reformed in a new configuration for the next task.

Such groups rely on clear objectives of the task and trust in each member rather than on a command structure to achieve their goal. This leads to dispensability: if necessary, one member can be replaced by another to fulfil the task. However, for the duration of the activity it is important that everyone knows the role they are assigned to, and fulfils it (see Chapter 15).

Employers no longer expect graduates to be knowledgeable only in their subject area but also to be able to demonstrate a range of 'core skills', including 'group skills' so that they can operate effectively (see Nicholson, 1990). This has been recognised in further education courses such as HND, HNC and BTec for some time. Recent initiatives in higher education, such as the Enterprise Learning Initiative, have encouraged the development of these skills in degree courses (see Entwistle, 1992).

 Activity 14.3

Can you identify any courses in which you practise any of the following core skills:
- communication
- problem solving
- group work?

You should be able to identify one course for at least one core skill area and probably courses for all three. It is useful to be able to reflect on how well you are developing these skills as well as your subject knowledge, as you will probably rely on them throughout your career.

The next section looks at another reason for working in a group – it helps you to learn!

Developing competent learning practices – learning by doing

This section looks at why group work is a more productive method of learning. So far, the reasons for working in groups have referred to the practices that you are likely to be faced with when you take up employment. This might seem a long way off and you may wonder what benefits group work has for you in the immediate future. Research has been carried out that suggests group work is beneficial. Methods that require you to be active, such as group work, actually help you learn more easily and more thoroughly than the traditional passive ways.

Kolb's model (see Figure 10.1 on page 33) is based on the premise that we learn more effectively by starting the learning process from a concrete experience rather than from an abstract concept. Yet in education we are often expected to learn in the reverse manner. We learn the theory and then apply it, sometimes not until we have left education.

Kolb's model is based on a cycle which includes active learning (participating in an activity) and passive learning (learning by non-participation in an activity, eg lectures, books). These provide both concrete and abstract experience. Kolb's model was described in detail in Chapter 10.

 Activity 14.4

An example of Kolb's cycle of learning might be as follows:

You are given a camera for your birthday. You have no knowledge of how to take professional photographs, but you decide to 'have a go'. You point the lens at a suitable object and press the button. When you receive your pictures, you observe their poor quality and reflect on the lack of understanding you have of photography. You decide to join a class or read a book in order to gain knowledge. When you have your new knowledge you buy another film for your camera and take some more pictures, this time testing out what you have learned.

You may have used your camera for the first time with a competent friend and, between you, you were able to learn more quickly the best method for taking photographs. Note how working in a group, as a class or with a friend, helped you to learn better.

Can you give an example of when you have experienced learning in Kolb's order?

You may or may not feel that you have experienced such a learning cycle. Either way, next time you are asked to 'have a go' before you understand the conceptual basis of the activity, you might like to reflect that you are learning in a Kolb manner and consider whether it is beneficial to you.

Conclusion

Now that you have considered what groups you belong to and how they assist you in your learning, read the next chapter to find out how groups work effectively.

15 How do groups work?

This chapter discusses how each of us interacts when we work together in a group. This includes taking on a role to complement each others' roles and communicating fully and clearly so that we understand one another.

Group dynamics: the roles people play

You may be able to choose your group or you may be allocated to one by your tutor. If you have the choice, what should you look for?
- people you like
- those with similar interests
- superbrains
- flatmates
- friends.

There are no hard and fast rules about this, but there is research evidence that successful teams have a mix of personalities.

Research by R. Meredith Belbin (1981) suggests that teams with high scorers on mental ability tests, which he called Apollo teams, did not perform well in group tasks. They tended to be argumentative, difficult to manage and destructive in debate. They also found it difficult to make decisions. So beware a team of 'superbrains'. He also found that teams with similar personalities did not perform well. So if you are like your friends, look around for different workmates.

Belbin's work indicated that there are eight key roles which successful teams need to fill:
- **a** Company worker
- **b** Chairman
- **c** Shaper
- **d** Plant
- **e** Resource investigator
- **f** Monitor-evaluator
- **g** Team worker
- **h** Completer-finisher.

Activity 15.1

Belbin's self-perception inventory

Belbin's inventory was developed as a means of giving group members a simple way of assessing their best team roles.

The inventory is set out in this activity to help you find out which role would suit you best. You will also find descriptions of the roles identified.

Although you may have a preferred role, it is likely that you can play other roles. Indeed you may need to if you discover that there is too much overlap of roles in your group.

Directions

For each of the following sections, distribute a total of ten points among the sentences which you think best describe your behaviour. These points may be distributed among several sentences; in extreme cases they might be spread among all the sentences or ten points may be given to a single sentence. Enter the points in the table on page 63.

1 What I believe I can contribute to a team

a I think I can quickly see and take advantage of new opportunities.

b I can work well with a very wide range of people.

c Producing ideas is one of my natural assets.

d My ability rests in being able to draw people out whenever I detect they have something of value to contribute to group objectives.

e My capacity to follow through has much to do with my personal effectiveness.

f I am ready to face temporary unpopularity if it leads to worthwhile results in the end.

g I am quick to sense what is likely to work in a situation with which I am familiar.

h I can offer a reasoned case for alternative courses of action without introducing bias or prejudice.

2 If I have a possible shortcoming in teamwork, it could be that

a I am not at ease unless meetings are well structured and controlled and generally well conducted.

b I am inclined to be too generous towards others who have a valid viewpoint that has not been given a proper airing.

c I have a tendency to talk a lot once the group gets on to new ideas.

d My objective outlook makes it difficult for me to join in readily and enthusiastically with colleagues.

e I am sometimes seen as forceful and authoritarian if there is a need to get something done.

f I find it difficult to lead from the front, perhaps because I am over responsive to group atmosphere.

g I am apt to get too caught up in ideas that occur to me and so lose track of what is happening.

h My colleagues tend to see me as worrying unnecessarily over detail and the possibility that things may go wrong.

3   When involved in a project with other people

a I have an aptitude for influencing people without pressurising them.

b My general vigilance prevents careless mistakes and omissions being made.

c I am ready to press for action to make sure that the meeting does not waste time or lose sight of the main objective.

d I can be counted on to contribute something original.

e I am always ready to back a good suggestion in the common interest.

f I am keen to look for the latest in new ideas and developments.

g I believe my capacity for cool judgement is appreciated by others.

h I can be relied upon to see that all essential work is organised.

4   My characteristic approach to group work is that

a I have a quiet interest in getting to know colleagues better.

b I am not reluctant to challenge the views of others or to hold a minority view myself.

c I can usually find a line of argument to refute unsound propositions.

d I think I have a talent for making things work once a plan has to be put into operation.

e I have a tendency to avoid the obvious and to come out with the unexpected.

f I bring a touch of perfectionism to any team job I undertake.

g I am ready to make use of contacts outside the group itself.

h While I am interested in all views, I have no hesitation in making up my mind once a decision has to be made.

5   I gain satisfaction in a job because

a I enjoy analysing situations and weighing up all the possible choices.

b I am interested in finding practical solutions to problems.

c I like to feel I am fostering good working relationships.

d I can have a strong influence on decisions.

e I can meet people who may have something new to offer.

f I can get people to agree on a necessary course of action.

g I feel in my element when I can give a task my full attention.

h I like to find a field that stretches my imagination.

6   **If I am given a difficult task suddenly with limited time and unfamiliar people**

a I would feel like retiring to a corner to devise a way out of the impasse before developing a line.

b I would be ready to work with the person who showed the most positive approach, however difficult s/he might be.

c I would find some way of reducing the size of the task by establishing what different individuals might best contribute.

d My natural sense of urgency would help to ensure that we did not fall behind schedule.

e I believe I would keep cool and maintain my capacity to think straight.

f I would retain a steadiness of purpose in spite of the pressures.

g I would be prepared to take a positive lead if I felt the group was making no progress.

h I would open up discussions with a view to stimulating new thoughts and getting something moving.

7   **With reference to the problems to which I am subject in working in groups**

a I am apt to show my impatience with those who are obstructing progress.

b Others may criticise me for being too analytical and insufficiently intuitive.

c My desire to ensure that work is done properly can hold up proceedings.

d I tend to get bored rather easily and rely on one or two stimulating members to spark me off.

e I find it difficult to get started unless the goals are clear.

f I am sometimes poor at explaining and clarifying complex points that occur to me.

g I am conscious of demanding from others the things I cannot do myself.

h I hesitate to get my points across when I run up against real opposition.

Points table for Belbin's self-perception inventory

Section / Item	a	b	c	d	e	f	g	h
1								
2								
3								
4								
5								
6								
7								

To interpret the inventory you should now look at the *analysis table* below. Transpose the scores taken from the points table above, entering them, section by section, in the analysis table. Then add up the points in each column to give a total team role distribution score.

Analysis table

Section / Item	CW		CH		SH		PL		RI		ME		TW		CF	
1	g		d		f		c		a		h		b		e	
2	a		b		e		g		c		d		f		h	
3	h		a		c		d		f		g		e		b	
4	d		h		b		e		g		c		a		f	
5	b		f		d		h		e		a		c		g	
6	f		c		g		a		h		e		b		d	
7	e		g		a		f		d		b		h		c	
Total																

Interpretation of total scores and further notes

The highest score on team role will indicate how best the respondent can make his or her mark in a management or project team. The next highest scores can denote back-up team roles towards which the individual should shift if for some reason there is less group need for a primary team role.

The two lowest scores in team role imply possible areas of weakness. But rather than attempting to reform in this area, the manager may be better advised to seek a colleague with complementary strengths.

Descriptions of the team roles are given in the *glossary table* on page 65. The titles of the team roles owe something both to historical factors and to the need to avoid the preconceptions associated with established alternatives. These could not be entirely overcome and can therefore be misread. For example the *Chairman* team-role refers to the characteristics of chairmen found in successful companies. In fact, some successful chairmen of industrial or commercial groups do not themselves adopt a typical *Chairman* stance, but make their mark as *Shapers* (where sharp or rigorous action is the order of the day) or as *Plants* (where the chairman's role is basically strategic).

Company worker or *Team worker* team roles have tended to be undervalued because of their titles. The former has been replaced in some firms by the title of *Implementer*, but there is much to be said for the *Company maker,* with its flavour of someone who acts as the backbone of the company. As an alternative to *Team worker* the terms *Team* and *Team workers* in the business and industrial world become *Chairmen* of their firms. In these cases, some aspects of their *Chairman* behaviour are learned, although other aspects of their style are likely to reflect their primary team role.

Experience with the self-perception inventory indicates that the most preferred team role for executives is *Shaper*, and the least preferred is *Completer*. We can therefore conjure up the image of the typical manager as good at initiating things, being pushy, outgoing and reactive, but weak in follow through. Such a conclusion should be treated with some reservation, however, because in every questionnaire there is a tendency for some responses to be more popular than others. It is useful therefore to see how individual respondents compare with executives in general.

Glossary table

Type	Symbol	Typical features	Positive qualities	Allowable weaknesses
Company worker	CW	Conservative, dutiful, predictable	Organising ability, practical common sense, hard working, self-disciplined	Lack of flexibility, unresponsiveness to unproven ideas
Chairman	CH	Calm, self-confident, controlled	A capacity for treating and welcoming all potential contributors on their merits and without prejudice. A strong sense of objectives	No more than ordinary in terms of intellect or creative ability
Shaper	SH	Highly strung, outgoing, dynamic	Drive and a readiness to challenge inertia, ineffectiveness, complacency or self-deception	Proneness to provocation, irritation and impatience
Plant	PL	Individualistic, serious-minded, unorthodox	Genius, imagination, intellect, knowledge	Up in the clouds, inclined to disregard practical details or protocol
Resource investigator	RI	Extroverted, enthusiastic, curious, communicative	A capacity for contacting people and exploring anything new. An ability to respond to challenge	Liable to lose interest once the initial fascination has passed
Monitor-evaluator	ME	Sober, unemotional, prudent	Judgement, discretion, hard-headedness	Lacks inspiration or the ability to motivate others
Team worker	TW	Socially-oriented, rather mild, sensitive	An ability to respond to people and to situations, and to promote team spirit	Indecisive at moments of crisis
Completer-finisher	CF	Painstaking, orderly, conscientious, anxious	A capacity for follow through. Perfectionism	A tendency to worry about small things. A reluctance to 'let go'

You should now have a better idea about the role you prefer to take in a group. When you next participate in a group activity remember what your preferred role is and try to develop the potential that this gives you.

Belbin focuses on how our personality moulds the roles we assume in groups. There are also more general roles that we need to take on in order to complete a group activity successfully. David Jaques (1992, page 34) has highlighted two such types of role:

a group building and maintenance roles – maintain group cohesiveness;

b group task roles – ensure completion of the project.

The point to remember is that your group will work better if you play different roles and maintain a balance between strategic interests and group maintenance.

Most groups need the following:

- **a leader** or **chair** to coordinate strategy and to give the group direction. Meetings will be more productive if you agree an agenda and stick to it;
- **a timekeeper** who can hold you to deadlines and keep your group meetings within specified time limits. If you play this role you need to take a firm line;
- **a note taker** to keep track of meetings. Try to photocopy notes of meetings so that everybody has a record;
- **a monitor** to check the progress and nudge things along if necessary;
- **a finisher** to tie up the ends. This may involve collating the final draft of a written report or setting up rehearsals if a presentation is required.

 Activity 15.2

If you are allocated to a group you could find out your preferred roles on the self-perception inventory in Activity 15.1. Alternatively you could try a SWOT analysis. (If you have not already read Part B: Managing your learning, turn to pages 35–36 now and find out what a SWOT analysis is.) The example below may help you.

strengths	**weaknesses**
Enjoy working in a group	Cannot word-process
Good on performance work	Find report writing difficult
	Not good on time management

opportunities	**threats**
This project may give me the	Deadline for project
chance to improve my	coincides with two other
research skills	assignments

Draw some SWOT templates and complete them for yourself individually and in your group.

The idea is to develop your strengths, make the most of your opportunities and turn your weaknesses into strengths and threats into opportunities. Look at the examples above. How might you do this?

Here are some suggestions.

How to turn weaknesses into strengths and threats into opportunities

This is not a simple matter, but by identifying the issues you know where to start.

a If you cannot word-process, make plans to learn. You may not be good enough for *this* project, but it is a skill you should have for the future.

b Your report writing skills will improve with practice. A group project gives you both the chance to tackle a small part of the report and the opportunity to work with those who are more proficient.

c If you are worried about completing several projects at once and feel that you need to sharpen up your time management skills, you need help. Are there tutors who could help you? Alternatively, study Part A: Time management, which will help you manage your programme more effectively.

 Activity 15.3

When you have done your SWOT analyses you may find that there are gaps in your group profile. Look at the following problems and write down your solutions.

What happens if:
- no leader has emerged?
- too many leaders have emerged?
- no one can word-process the report?
- a particular task is unfilled, eg timekeeper?

Make a note of your other issues.

Remember, when you are in employment your teams will not be perfect; you will have to compromise and adjust if you are going to survive and achieve your goals. You might like to compare your solutions with these.

Problem: no leader has emerged

Solution:

a Manage without one. This may work in some groups, particularly if they are small, but it may take you longer to complete the project.

b Identify the skills involved and match them to your SWOT analysis. Negotiate with those who come closest to the roles that need to be filled.

c Divide the project up and have one leader to organise the written element and another to plan the presentation. Watch that it doesn't get too fragmented.

Problem: too many leaders have emerged

Solution:

This could be difficult if the group gets pulled in several directions at once. Try to negotiate a solution. You may opt for **b** or **c** above. Remember there will be other opportunities to try out roles in future group activities.

Problem: no one can word-process the report

Solution:

a Decide if there is time or opportunity for any group members to learn.

b Consider alternatives – relatives, friends or a more contractual (and expensive!) arrangement. Sort it out early!

Problem: we're not strong on time management skills – no one wants to take on the role of timekeeper

Solution:

a Decide if the role is vital to the group – this one usually is.

b Look at the skills of the group and try to negotiate who might take it on – perhaps in addition to another role. In small groups you may need to take on several roles at once. Make sure you are clear at the outset what your responsibilities entail.

c Look for materials to help you. In this case you could have a look at Part A: Time management in this book. Make sure each group member reads it.

Group dynamics: communication

Working in groups requires good interpersonal communication. If your group is to perform successfully you must communicate with each other in order to agree the aims of the task and to form and maintain a cohesiveness. This will ensure that the momentum for the task is sustained.

This section will describe the communication process and will help you identify problems and then make suggestions as to possible solutions. It will address these issues in the following sub-sections:

The function of communication in group dynamics

a Communication strategies

b Conveying the message.

Reasons and solutions for communication failure

   a Giving messages
   b Receiving messages
   c Taking turns to communicate.

The function of communication in group dynamics

a Communication strategies

The two roles that have been shown to be essential in successful groups are those of task and maintenance. The task role ensures the completion of the project; the maintenance role controls group cohesion. Both roles adopt communication strategies to fulfil their function. These include *task behaviour* and *maintenance behaviour*.

Task behaviour, eg:
- discussing with each other what objectives you need to agree upon to complete the task successfully;
- drawing up a timetable of tasks to be done by certain group members.

 Activity 15.4

   Can you think of any more strategies?

Here are some further suggestions:
- someone to take notes at meetings to ensure accurate records of progress are kept;
- someone who agrees to take charge of booking equipment, eg tape recorders/ video cameras for interviewing.

Maintenance behaviour, eg:
- regular meetings to discuss everyone's progress;
- praising work done by each other.

 Activity 15.5

Can you think of any more strategies?

Here are some further suggestions:
- sharing telephone numbers and addresses to keep in regular contact;
- encouraging each other to make suggestions to improve progress.

Whenever you consider how effectively your group is communicating, it is useful to remember that both task and maintenance roles need to be addressed.

b   Conveying the message

Once strategies have been agreed that will further the group work, the content and process of the communication function need to be considered. These can be discussed under the topics of *what is communicated* and *how it is communicated*.

What is communicated

This refers to the content of the message. It can be thoughts about the task or the group activity, or it can be feelings about either. Thoughts are often more easily expressed and understood than feelings, which can be difficult to express and can be misunderstood by the listener.

How it is communicated

The process of communicating has been the focus of a particular theoretical debate for many decades. Models of communication have become increasingly more complex. One of the simplest, developed by Shannon and Weaver (1949), represents communication as a linear process in which information is *encoded* by a *sender*, transmitted through a *channel* and *decoded* by a *receiver*.

This model has been criticised for its linear nature and its emphasis on the sender rather than on the receiver. Its prime interest lies in the technical expertise of sending messages rather than the *meaning* both encoded and decoded in the message. Later models recognise communication as an interpersonal relationship and include the element of *feedback* from the receiver to the sender. They also consider the importance of cultural and social influences that cannot be divorced from the communication process. Together these theories offer you a framework within which to analyse your group communication.

The process by which a message is communicated relies on both *verbal* and *non-verbal* cues.

Verbal cues can convey not only information but also emotions and feelings, for example through sarcasm or irony. They include the tone, inflection and clarity of the voice and the semantics used.

Non-verbal cues can communicate various messages:
- your emotional state;
- your self-image, this may be culturally determined, eg deference shown by lowered eyes;
- your relationship, eg forms of greetings.

Non-verbal cues include facial expressions, posture and gestures, as well as the use of personal space and the amount of body contact.

Communication is not a one-way activity and so the recipient of the message must be included in the communication process. This requires the skills of both *listening* and giving *feedback*.

Listening
This should be an *active* role. You should:
- concentrate on what is being said;
- identify the key points;
- compare what is being said with your own thoughts.

Do not just concentrate on waiting for a chance to intervene.

Feedback
Check that you have understood the message, eg
'So you think we need to distribute 100 questionnaires?'

Reflect on the message by answering, eg
'I agree. I think that's a good idea.'

Encourage more development of the conversation, eg
'That sounds interesting. Can you tell me more about your methods for collecting data?'

A recap on the function of communication in group dynamics
- Communication helps to support the task and maintenance roles in groups.
- It is important to identify what and how to communicate.
- Communication is a two-way process and the recipient should listen actively and give constructive feedback.

Reasons and solutions for communication failure

One of the most common reasons for group failure is non-communication. The reasons for this may be due to:
- a breakdown in the system of conveying a message between the speaker and the receiver. The speaker may not form the message clearly or use appropriate language; there may be interference as the message is transmitted, or the receiver may not be listening carefully;
- a breakdown in understanding the meaning of the message. The words may be heard clearly, but if the speaker and receiver do not share the same language, which can include jargon and slang, the meaning will be lost and communication will not have taken place. Some language theorists would go

further and argue that unless speaker and receiver share the same experiences of life they cannot fully communicate.

a Giving messages

The next activity will give you the opportunity to see whether you are able to avoid these breakdowns in communication and, if not, to discuss ways of combating them. The objective is to see how easy it is to communicate instructions and to receive them and put them into practice.

 Activity 15.6

The activity requires you to work in pairs. You will need two work surfaces, two chairs, a pair of scissors and Appendix 1 on page 80.

Instructions
Trace and cut out the shapes in Appendix 1 twice. Each of you should take a set of shapes and sit back to back, each facing a work surface. One of you should arrange the shapes in a random pattern and then give instructions to your partner to copy your pattern. Your partner must not turn around or ask questions. When your partner feels that s/he has finished, you may reveal your pattern.

When you have done this, continue with the activity. Now you should spend time discussing the process. The following prompts may be helpful:

- Was it easy to give/receive information?
- Did the speaker use understandable language to describe the pattern?
- Did the listener want to ask questions to gain more information?
- Did the speaker find it difficult to know when to proceed without verbal or non-verbal cues from the listener?
- Did the listener feel that the speaker was trying to help him/her in the task? If so, how?
- Did your sitting positions affect your relationship?

Now write down whether these issues are related to *task* or *maintenance* roles.

If the results of the activity were not very successful, try to identify the *problems* and suggest *solutions* to them.

You might have identified the following problems; see if you agree with the solutions.

Problem	Solution
Speaker did not set any physical boundaries to the area s/he was working in.	Speaker should give measurements and geometric planes, eg 'The pattern is formed in an area 2' x 1'. The first shape is a triangle, with the right-angle placed in the upper left-hand corner of the area.'
Speaker used unfamiliar language.	'An isosceles triangle has two equal sides.'
Speaker could not be heard clearly.	Speaker should move his/her head to the side and project his/her voice, slowly enunciating each syllable.
Speaker described the pattern as unconnected and meaningless . shapes.	Compare the pattern to something the listener has experience of, eg 'It looks like a cat!'

b Receiving messages

Successful communication also requires skills in listening and giving feedback. The next activity will help you look at your skills in these areas.

 Activity 15.7

Instructions
This activity requires three people: a speaker, listener and observer. The speaker and listener should sit opposite each other and the observer should sit close enough to watch the other two without being intrusive.

The speaker's role: spend a few minutes thinking about a recent event in your life that you feel deserves a sympathetic ear. This might be the experience of your last exam, shrinking your best T-shirt or finding that you had less money in your bank account than you thought! Relate it to the listener with lots of emotion, hoping to gain his/her sympathy.

The listener's role: you should listen sympathetically and give supportive feedback to the speaker.

The observer's role: complete Appendix 2: Triad checklist on page 81.

When the speaker and listener have completed their conversation, the observer should discuss the comments made on the Triad checklist. All participants should discuss how effective the listening and feedback skills were. You can compare them with the suggestions made in **b Conveying the message** on page 70.

There are further skills in giving feedback when you are placed in a supportive relationship. In your group you may need to disagree with and criticise each other at the same time as retaining the group's cohesion. The following suggestions for giving positive feedback can help:

- describe what you have experienced rather than evaluate it;
- be supportive and constructive rather than critical;
- choose to discuss behaviour that the person can alter;
- ask for feedback rather than wait for it to be offered;
- be specific rather than general.

c Taking turns to communicate

We have discussed the importance of giving and receiving messages as part of successful communication. In a group everyone needs both to give and receive messages regularly so that there is a balance of decision making and responsibility. In any group there are people who are confident to speak and those who are frightened to do so. A successful group will encourage all its members to speak, but this needs building up through both individual and group awareness.

Individual

Research has shown that after a certain length of time it is difficult to break into a conversation. Next time you are sitting in a seminar or tutorial see if it becomes more difficult to start speaking the later you break into the discussion. The following time try to speak as soon as possible and see if you feel more relaxed during the rest of the seminar.

Group

Often there are people who dominate discussion in groups and those who say nothing. Those who talk a lot may not necessarily be over confident. They may dislike silences and feel guilty if they do not support the tutor by saying something. They may not feel that they have a very important contribution, but are not embarrassed to 'have a go at offering a suggestion'. In a group discussion it is important to have a reasonable balance between speakers. If you feel that you always contribute more than others, ask another member of the group to add to your comment. Sometimes people are grateful for being given these cues. You could suggest that you all make one comment each so that everyone speaks and no one feels they have been singled out.

You could investigate how often group members speak by drawing up a **participation chart** (Figure 15.1). In your next discussion meeting an elected observer should draw a diagram, as below, with each member of the group represented by a circle. Each time they talk, the observer draws a line from them to whoever they speak to, or whoever takes up their point. This diagram should help the group to recognise where there is a communication imbalance and to try to rectify it. The activity may highlight the emergence of a leader. Refer back to the solutions following Activity 15.3 if you need to.

Figure 15.1: Participation chart

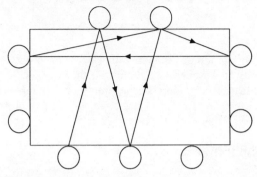

Conclusion

You should now be aware that you have at least one preferred role that you perform when working in a group, maybe more! The communication activities should have made you aware of the many pitfalls of not communicating competently. This knowledge should help you to contribute more effectively and to understand your fellow team members more fully. You now need to consider the last piece of the group work jigsaw. You each have a role to play. Now you need to recognise that there is a process to go through, sometimes slowly, in order to form your group. Turn to the next chapter to find out what the stages are in forming a group.

16 What stages do groups go through?

Introduction

You might think that forming a group was no more difficult than choosing to work with some of your best friends. However, when you work together in a specific group activity your relationship with each other must become professional. Before this can be achieved, the group may go through certain stages. Consider whether Adair's suggestions below fit your own experience of group work.

Adair's stages in group formation

Adair draws on the movement known as *group dynamics,* which is concerned with why groups behave in particular ways. This offers various suggestions for how groups are formed and how they develop over time. The formation of some groups can be represented as a spiral, other groups form with sudden movements forward and then have periods with no change. Whatever variant of formation each group exhibits, Adair suggests that they all pass through four sequential stages of development. These stages may be longer or shorter for each group, but all groups will need to experience them. Figure 16.1 shows the four stages that Adair identifies. They are *forming, storming, norming* and *performing.*

Figure 16.1: Adair's stages

	Group structure	Task activity
Forming	Considerable anxiety, testing to discover the nature of the situation, what help can be expected from leader or convenor and what behaviour will or will not be appropriate.	What is the task? Members seek the answers to that basic question, together with knowledge of the rules and the methods to be employed.
Storming	Conflict emerges between sub-groups; the authority and/or competence of the leader is challenged. Opinions polarise. Individuals react against efforts of the leader or group to control them.	The value and feasibility of the task is questioned. People react emotionally against its demands.
Norming	The group begins to harmonise; it experiences group cohesion or unity for the first time. Norms emerge as those in conflict are reconciled and resistance is overcome. Mutual support develops.	Cooperation on the task begins; plans are made and work standards laid down. Communication of views and feelings develops.
Performing	The group structures itself or accepts a structure which fits most appropriately its common task. Roles are seen in terms functional to the task and flexibility between them develops.	Constructive work on the task surges ahead; progress is experienced as more of the group's energy is applied to being effective in the area of their common task.

Activity 16.1

Read figure 16.1 again and answer the following questions:

Think of a group that you have recently been involved with. Considering each stage of its development, can you recall any evidence of these stages?

a Forming
- What was the task?
- Did you all share the same expectations of the task?
- Did you all have the same attitude to working in a group?

b Storming
- Was there any conflict in the group?
- Did you all agree on the means of carrying out the task?
- Did you have a leader and was his/her authority challenged?

c Norming
- Did you move on to agree methods of working?
- Did you have a common goal?
- Did you cooperate with each other?

d Performing
- Did everyone take on a functional role to achieve the task?
- Did you work constructively and efficiently?
- Did the group's activity focus on fulfilling the task?

You have now analysed your group's formation using Adair's theory. This should give you a good idea as to whether it is progressing well towards being an effective group – or maybe it has already arrived at the performing stage. If so, congratulations! Many groups remain at the storming stage and find it difficult to achieve their goals.

If your group is just beginning to form, Adair's comments should help you to recognise the issues which may either help or hinder you from progressing to the next stage. It would be useful to discuss with your group members how best to move forward.

17 Conclusion

This part of the book has taken you through the processes involved in beginning to work in a group. Your task now is to put it into practice.

Remember the key points:

- Working practices in education and the world of work are increasingly emphasising group and team work as an efficient and effective method of achieving desired end results.

- Working in a group emphasises 'active' ways of learning that lead to a deeper understanding of the topic being studied.

- Groups should be made up of people with different roles. Belbin suggests that there are eight key roles needed for successful teams.

- You probably have a preferred role to play in a group.

- Effective communication is essential for a group to be successful.

- Groups will go through stages of development before they 'perform' together successfully.

If you are now going to begin working on a group project, the final part, Managing your group project, will give you hints on how to plan your project.

Best of luck!

18 Bibliography

Adair, J. (1989) *Effective team building*, London, Gower.

Belbin, R. M. (1981) *Management teams – why they succeed or fail*, London, Butterworth Heinemann.

Entwistle, N. (1992) *The impact of teaching on learning outcomes in higher education*, Sheffield, CVCP.

Handy, C. and Aitken, R. (1986) *Understanding schools as organisations*, Harmondsworth, Penguin.

Jaques, D. (1992) *Learning in groups*, London, Kogan Page.

Kolb, D. A. *et al.* (1984) *Organisational psychology* (4th ed.), London, Prentice Hall.

Nicholson, B. (1990) *Towards a skills revolution: the report of the CBI vocational education and training task force*, Swindon, ACFHE.

Shannon, C. and Weaver, W. (1949) *The mathematical theory of communication*, Champaign, University of Illinois.

Sykes, J. B. (1976) *The Concise Oxford Dictionary* (6th ed.), Oxford, OUP.

Appendix 1: Communication activity

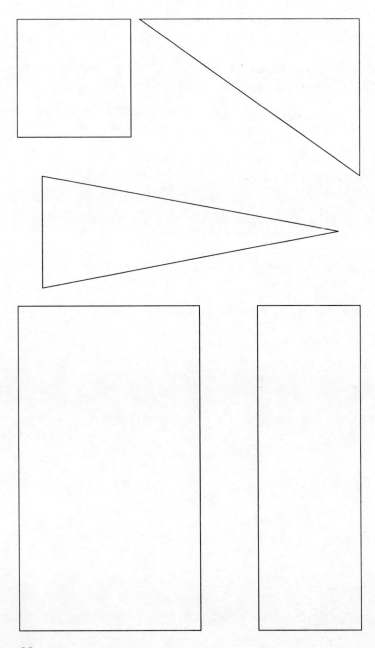

Appendix 2: Triad checklist

Observation

Did the speaker:

- Give positive body language?
- Look at the listener?
- Use 'tags' to encourage feedback?
- Try to link the listener to the experience of the story?

Any other positive/negative communication?

Did the listener:

- Show interest through body language?
- Look at the speaker?
- Make encouraging remarks?
- Show understanding of experience?

Any other positive/negative communication?

Part D: Managing your group project

Introduction

Projects are a feature of many courses and you may be expected to produce one individually or as part of a group. This part looks at how you handle a group project.

Objectives

The aim of this part is to develop your skills in group project management. When you have read it through and done the exercises you should be able to:
- plan and produce a group project to a given deadline;
- evaluate the processes involved in producing the group project;
- evaluate the project itself.

As you are working in a group you should have read **Part C: Working in groups.**

A project is a directed piece of work which will be assessed as part of your course. You will normally be given guidelines (a project brief) to help you complete it. These guidelines could be prescriptive (indicating what you must do) or they could be more open, allowing you greater freedom in the way you tackle the project.

A group project, as its name suggests, involves you working in a team to complete the task. This is becoming a common approach in higher education as it provides good preparation for employment – and for life!

19 How to manage your group project

Planning your project

There are four main concerns in planning your project which will be discussed in this chapter:
- Formulating aims;
- Setting clear objectives;
- Establishing needs and constraints;
- Devising a strategy.

Formulating aims

The *aims* of the project indicate what you are planning to achieve when the project is completed. You will find it more useful if your aims are specific and take into account your resources. The following examples will indicate how you might start with general aims, but then focus them on something more specific and useful to the project team.

Stage 1
You have decided as a group that the aim of the project is to report on the financial position of students. Do you have the resources to go beyond your own university? If not, you need to make your aim more specific.

Stage 2
The aim of the project is to report on the financial position of students at your own university or college. Do you need to include all categories of students in your research, or should you concentrate on particular groups? You may decide to consider only non-fee-paying undergraduates (this is the majority, but would exclude part-time students, overseas entrants and some other groups). You could now refine your aims still further.

Stage 3
The aim of the project is to report on the financial position of non-fee-paying undergraduates at ... (name of college or university).

Setting clear objectives

These are the steps which, when achieved, will allow you to recognise when you have reached your aim.

- Objectives usually should be measurable or quantifiable, eg:
  - to calculate the number of students who have received a student loan;
  - to investigate the number of students in paid employment in term time;
  - to calculate the number of students who are millionaires.

- Objectives should also be specific.

- Objectives can represent progressive milestones in a project. As you achieve one you move on to the next, eg:
  - an early objective would be 'to investigate ...'
  - a later one would be 'to review the findings ...'

 Activity 19.1

This will give you an opportunity to develop the aims and objectives of your project.

    a Using your project guidelines, outline the aim of your group project. Remember this is what you are planning to achieve.

    b Do you need to revise this to make it more specific?

Now focus on listing the objectives. Remember these are the steps which, when achieved, will allow you to recognise that you have achieved your aims.

Establishing needs and constraints

In order to achieve your objectives you must decide what needs and constraints the group has, eg:

- Will you require any resources?
- Do you need a tape recorder if you are carrying out interviews?
- Are you confined to particular times of the day to work on your project?

Devising a strategy

To manage your project you should be aware of three forms of measurement: *quality*, *time* and *cost*.

You should decide which of these has priority (though they are all linked) and then devise a strategy to work towards it. For example, you may want to gain a high mark for your project and therefore quality will be very important. However, you may not be able to afford to pay for professional presentation materials which will affect the overall quality, and in fact the final overriding priority might be the time limit set by your tutor.

To devise your strategy there are a number of questions you should ask yourselves.

    a How many people are in the group?

    b What common time do you have together?

    c How much time do you have?

    d Are resources available on a regular basis?

    e What costs can we incur?

The next stage is to work out all the necessary steps or tasks to achieve your objectives.

Let's take the example given on page 83 and identify some of the tasks involved. The aim of the project is to report on the financial position of non-fee paying undergraduates at … (name of college or university).

The project could involve the following tasks:
- identification of a random sample of non-fee-paying students;
- library search of the literature on the financial position of students;
- formulation of a questionnaire for students to complete;
- analysis of the research findings;
- library search of the literature on research methods;
- decision on which research methods to use for the project;
- writing up the aims, literature search, research methods sections;
- writing up the review of the findings and the recommendations;
- distribution and collection of questionnaires;
- collating/checking the report and handing it in by deadline.

Once you have identified all of the tasks you need to work out:
a the activities involved; and
b the order in which they should be completed.

The next two activities will help you with this.

 Activity 19.2

List all of the tasks which you will need to complete to achieve your objective and identify what needs to be done, eg:

Task	**Activity**
Library search of the available literature on the financial position of students	Library research for a maximum of three hours

---

When you have identified the steps you will need to put them into a network diagram to work out the critical path.

Network diagram
This sets out all the tasks that need to be done in a particular order and at specific times so that the project may be completed on time. It also gives you control over the project.

The network diagram below gives an example to copy. You will notice that the tasks identified above have now been put into a sequence. The critical path runs from 1 to 7. Low number tasks precede high numbers but, as you are working in a group, some tasks can be arranged in parallel, eg **1** and **1a** can be done at the same time, but they must be finished before you go on to **2**.

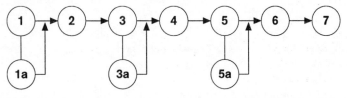

Key

1 Library search of literature on the financial position of students.
1a Library search of the literature on research methods.
2 Decision on which research methods to use for the project.
3 Identification of a random sample of non-fee-paying students.
3a Formulation of a questionnaire for students to complete.
4 Distribution and collection of questionnaires.
5 Writing up the aims, literature search, research methods sections.
5a Analysis of the research findings.
6 Writing up the review of the findings and the recommendations.
7 Collating/checking the report and handing it in by deadline.

 Activity 19.3

Now it's your turn. The first stage is to list all the tasks to be done. You will have done this already in Activity 19.2, but you may wish to amend your list.

Now number the tasks. If you think that two or more can be completed at the same time use the same number and add a letter as in the example above. Bear in mind the time allowance you identified in the previous activity. You may find it easier to put each task on to individual pieces of paper and move them around until you get the most logical sequence.

Now draw the diagram. This will give you a tight plan to work from. If a task has to be moved or takes longer than expected, you should recalculate the time allowance or try to rearrange other tasks to gain lost time.

Make sure everyone has a copy of the diagram and that they know what the numbers mean.

Activity 19.4

When you are about to begin your project, complete the following sections:
- Title of project
- Aims
- Objectives
- Needs/constraints
- Tasks/activities
- Network diagram.

Organising your project

This section will try to help you organise your activities so as to avoid the common pitfalls. For example, if one of your group 'disappears' you will need to devise a strategy to cope. The issues will be considered in the following order:
- Getting established
- Anticipating problems
- Getting off to a good start
- Managing your time
- Allocating the tasks
- Choreographing your activities.

Getting established

This will help when you are working in a group. Many groups fail because they are not set up properly. You need to get to know each other early on in the project and to establish some ground rules for the group.

At the start you are likely to be a collection of individuals engaged on a project. You have to work at becoming a group, which involves individuals working together. Your tutors may help you with this, but you will probably be left to your own resources. How you start to organise yourselves will depend on whether you already know each other. If not, introductions are a first step. Spend some time talking about yourselves, what you are good at, what you can contribute, what you hate to do, etc. You'll get to know each other better if you get involved in some activity together. This could be a social activity, like meeting in a pub or coffee bar, or something structured around the project.

Before you get too set in your ideas about the task in hand you could try 'brainstorming' some aspect of the group project, for example its needs and constraints. Brainstorming enables you to collect ideas quickly. Usually one of the group writes everything down on a large sheet of paper so that everyone can see what is being

87

developed. You can sort and sift it later. You should establish some ground rules for the brainstorm; this will be good practice for the project itself.

Rules that might help you when brainstorming include:
- setting a time limit and allocating a 'timekeeper' to see that you stick to it;
- allowing everything to be included – no matter how outlandish;
- encouraging everyone to participate;
- going for quantity, not quality;
- letting the group build up points from those already written down.

You then need to establish some ground rules for your project. One way of doing this is to identify things that might go wrong.

Anticipating problems

 ### Activity 19.5

As an alternative to brainstorming try the 30-second theatre game. Everyone is asked to think about the worst thing that could happen to a group project and then write it down anonymously. The responses are then collected up and the group acts out each scenario for 30 seconds. Some solutions should emerge which will help with future problems.

Your 'worst situations' might have included some of the following:
- We don't know each other.
- Some of the group don't pull their weight.
- We are not clear who is going to do what.
- We don't know how to contact each other.
- We don't stick to deadlines.
- We don't arrange regular meetings.
- We won't have time to bring all the parts of the report together and make it into one coherent piece of work.
- We won't have time to rehearse our presentation.
- One of the group was ill and no one found out until the last minute.
- We disagreed so much at the start that it took ages to get going.
- We realised too late that none of us could word-process.
- Everyone talks, but no one listens.

The next section offers some help with possible solutions.

Getting off to a good start

Look again at why groups might experience difficulties. Some problems might be avoided if you set ground rules early on. Here are examples which address some of the problems identified above:

a Decide how you will contact each other. You might exchange telephone numbers, use student notice-boards or make contact via pigeon-holes. Make sure everyone is clear on the procedures.

b Arrange to meet socially soon – even the student coffee bar would get you started.

c Establish how you will find out if one of the group is ill. This is vital.

d Make sure that you are clear what is required by your tutors; check the assessment criteria and keep these in mind.

e Agree whether you are expected to attend all meetings; you may need some with the whole group and some for task-specific groups.

f Agree that all criticism will be constructive.

g Agree to help each other out if anyone is having difficulty – it is a team effort after all!

 Activity 19.6

Now make a note of other ground rules that you want to include.

Managing your time

Many groups start slowly and leave insufficient time to rehearse their presentation and write up their report collaboratively. Your ability to meet deadlines is crucial and there are often severe penalties if your assignment is late. You will need to think about this as a group as well as for yourself. The following suggestions may help.

a Work backwards from your hand-in date.

b Assess how much time you will need to rehearse a presentation if one is required.

c Work out how you are going to present your report and how long it will take.

d Set up regular meetings and agree the location. Write the arrangements down and make sure everyone has a copy. Agree a meeting after the handing-in date to evaluate your project (you could include a social event to provide an incentive).

e Agree the start and finish times of meetings and stick to them. Set an agenda. People are more likely to attend if the meetings are well run.

f Establish priorities, both for yourself and for the group.

g Decide how you will cope as a group if one (or more) of you is falling behind.

Allocating the tasks

The size of the group will influence how you allocate tasks. If you are working in pairs or in a small group you will need to divide up the tasks, but the mechanism is likely to be less formal. Once you get to groups of around five or more you do need to ensure that a fair distribution of tasks occurs and that everyone is clear about the division of responsibilities.

You will find it easier to allocate the tasks if you have already sorted out the roles. You will need to look back at Part C: Working in groups, to make sense of the following section. You will then be able to structure your meetings with a chair, timekeeper, monitor (that is progress chaser) etc.

You will have identified the tasks under Devising a strategy (pages 84–5). Some tasks will be suitable for individuals, others for small sub-groups. There may be some disagreement among your group on this. Disagreement is no bad thing, as long as it is constructive and objective. Groups that are reluctant to debate and challenge are unlikely to be creative and dynamic. Everyone should have the chance to consider and to influence the options. Clearly, if the disagreement goes on for too long it will be counterproductive. This is where the chair and timekeeper should try to keep you to deadlines.

 Activity 19.7

SWOT analysis

If you have not already done a SWOT analysis, try one (see Activity 10.2 on pages 35–6). It may help you to identify where your strengths and weaknesses lie. You need to try to turn the weaknesses into strengths, and the threats into opportunities.

You may be able to identify those who could take the lead in certain areas, eg doing library research, developing a questionnaire, writing up the report, making a video. Check that everyone is clear about:
• what they are expected to do; and
• when they are expected to do it.

To avoid confusion, write this down and copy it for everyone.

Choreographing your activities

The more you all know about the project, the more you can ensure that the component parts fit together for the final report or presentation. You should not be able to see the joins.

a 'The show must go on ...'

One of the main reasons that groups fail is that one member of the group does not complete their part of the task. Clearly it would be impractical to have an 'understudy' for every task, but as a group you need to be able to identify problems early on and deal with them.

b What to look out for

- non-attendance at meetings – particularly if no messages of apology are sent;
- difficulty in contacting the person concerned;
- failure to meet deadlines;
- persistent excuses.

c What should you do?

If you are failing to make contact, check with your tutor to see if the student is ill.

If you are getting anxious about the deadlines, failure to produce work, persistent excuses, non-attendance at meetings:
- get your *monitor* to chase it up (if the monitor is the problem another group member will need to take this on);
- offer support;
- write to express the group's concern and indicate what you are planning to do. Keep a copy and make sure that you date it;
- other group members should be prepared to take on the tasks. Don't leave it too long or your project might fail.

If you *are* required to make a presentation, the more you rehearse the better. Coerce friends to give you critical feedback. This will ensure that your presentation reflects your group activity (not individual bits strung together at the last minute) and will enable you to cope more effectively if any of your group are absent. If one of your group is ill, check the procedures with your tutor. You may be able to postpone the presentation if you present a medical certificate.

Doing your project

There will be considerable variations according to your subject area and the project brief you are following. This section will outline some basic rules.

Choosing your research topic

For some projects you may not have much choice, as your brief will specify the task to be completed. For others you may be given more freedom. Try to negotiate a topic that the group can tackle and for which resources are available.

Doing your literature search

For most projects there will be existing literature that you should try to read before you start. You may find it helpful for one or more of your group to embark on this fairly quickly to establish some parameters for your study. Remember to keep a note of full references as you go along. You can waste a lot of time if you have to chase them up at the end.

Choosing your research methods

For some projects you may need to do some practical research. This may be to test an hypothesis (an idea you have which may be tested empirically). Some projects will require access to laboratories or workshops for experimental research. For others you will need to investigate a sample of the population using interviews or questionnaires.

Presenting your project

Most projects require a written report. This may include a log of the group's activities. Even if you are not required to produce one it may help with your evaluation. There will probably be guidelines on the written report. Follow them. You may be required to make a group presentation. Remember to allow enough time to proof-read the report *after* you have used a spell check and to rehearse the presentation. Part A of this book, Time management, will help.

Referencing your materials

At the end of your study you should include references to all of the materials you have used. This will be mainly books and articles, but there can be other sources. Your tutors may prefer a particular style of citation. Check this with them. This book uses the *Harvard* system. The main rule is to be consistent and to make sure that everyone in the group is operating with the same style. Agree this at the start.

If you copy out a quotation you must credit the author. If you fail to do so you are plagiarising his/her work, ie you are passing it off as your own. You must write everything in your own words. If you are paraphrasing someone else's point you must indicate who wrote it and where it can be found. Failure to do so is cheating and there are heavy penalties. Many tutors give zero for plagiarised work, and some students get thrown out!

20 How to evaluate your project

You should try to evaluate the *process* and the *product* of your project:
- the *process* will enable you to look back at how you worked as a group;
- the *product* will enable you to evaluate the end products of the project.

Evaluating the process

 Activity 20.1

Were there advantages and disadvantages of working in this group? Write them down. You should also consider the part you played in the team.

a List the advantages and disadvantages.

b Now suggest ways forward in the future.

 Activity 20.2

Look back at your network diagram (Chapter 19, page 86). Draw a new one which would improve your project.

 Activity 20.3

Which roles did the group members play? Write down your reflections on this, then make some suggestions on how things could be improved in the future.

 Activity 20.4

Look back at Chapter 19, page 88, where we considered the 'worst situations' and the main reasons why groups might fail.

Did you fall into any of these traps? If so, write them down and then suggest how to improve next time.

Eg Our group was not good at:

Next time we must:

Evaluating the product

 Activity 20.5

    a Were you satisfied with the outcome of the project?
    b Did it meet the assessment criteria set?
    c Were there ways in which it could be improved?
    d What mark/feedback did you receive?
    e How might you improve next time?

If you are not sure about this you should see your tutor to get some feedback.

Copy out Activity 20.5 for use with other projects. It will enable you to keep a check on your own progress with group projects.

21 Bibliography

Belbin, R. M. (1981) *Management teams – why they succeed or fail*, London, Butterworth Heinemann.

Gibbs, G. (1992) *Independent learning with more students*, Oxonian Rewley Press.

Also available from Kogan Page